SCHOLASTIC 2024 BOOK OF WORLD RECORDS

BY
CYNTHIA O'BRIEN
ABIGAIL MITCHELL
MICHAEL BRIGHT
DONALD SOMMERVILLE
ANTONIA VAN DER MEER
CHRIS HAWKES

If you purchased this book without a cover, you should be aware that this book is stolen property. It was reported as "unsold and destroyed" to the publisher, and neither the author nor the publisher has received any payment for this "stripped book."

Copyright © 2023 by Scholastic Inc.

All rights reserved. Published by Scholastic Inc., *Publishers since 1920*. SCHOLASTIC and associated logos are trademarks and/or registered trademarks of Scholastic Inc.

Due to this book's publication date, the majority of statistics are current as of February 2023. The publisher does not have any control over and does not assume any responsibility for author or third-party websites or their content.

No part of this publication may be reproduced, stored in a retrieval system, or transmitted in any form or by any means, electronic, mechanical, photocopying, recording, or otherwise, without written permission of the publisher. For information regarding permission, write to Scholastic Inc., Attention: Permissions Department, 557 Broadway, New York, NY 10012.

This book was created and produced by Toucan Books Limited.
Text: Cynthia O'Brien, Abigail Mitchell, Michael Bright, Donald Sommerville, Antonia van der Meer, Chris Hawkes
Designer: Lee Riches
Editor: Anna Southgate
Proofreader: Marilyn Knowlton
Index: Marie Lorimer
Toucan would like to thank Cian O'Day
for picture research.

ISBN 978-1-339-01311-4

10 9 8 7 6 5 4 3 2   23 24 25 26 27

Printed in the U.S.A.   40

First printing, 2023

CONTENTS

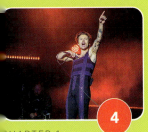

CHAPTER 1
MUSIC MAKERS — 4

CHAPTER 2
SCREEN & STAGE — 22

CHAPTER 3
ON THE MOVE — 46

CHAPTER 4
SUPER STRUCTURES — 62

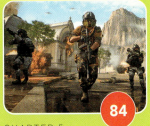

CHAPTER 5
HIGH TECH — 84

CHAPTER 6
AMAZING ANIMALS — 110

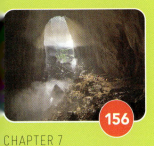

CHAPTER 7
INCREDIBLE EARTH — 156

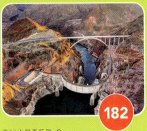

CHAPTER 8
STATE STATS — 182

CHAPTER 9
SPORTS STARS — 236

278 Index
285 Photo Credits

CHAPTER 1
MUSIC MAKERS

MUSIC MAKERS
TRENDING

IT'S GOT THE JUICE
CORN KID GOES VIRAL

Seven-year-old Tariq made headlines in August 2022 when a video of him expressing his love for corn went viral on TikTok. In the original clip, he was being interviewed by Web series host Julian Shapiro-Barnum at the New York food festival Smorgasburg, but his wide-eyed enthusiasm soon caught the attention of The Gregory Brothers, a musical quartet, who remixed Tariq's words into a catchy song. "It's Corn" was watched more than 1.6 million times in its first week on YouTube, becoming an instant hit!

STRANGER SONGS
SHOW INSPIRES KATE BUSH REVIVAL

Netflix's *Stranger Things* is set in the 1980s and is known for its throwback soundtrack. One song in season four really caused a stir, when the creators used Kate Bush's 1985 hit "Running Up That Hill" in one of its most dramatic scenes. Sadie Sink's character, Max, is listening to the song while confronting the season's main villain. Kate Bush earned an estimated $2.3 million from the feature and made it to no. 3 on the *Billboard* Top 10.

EMOTIONAL PERFORMANCE
BTS TAKE THE STAGE BEFORE HIATUS

K-pop's record-breaking boy band went big at their first concert after announcing their hiatus. Around 50,000 people chosen by lottery watched their free two-hour "Yet to Come in Busan" show, live at Busan Asiad Main Stadium. The performance included the song "Ma City," a tribute to Busan, the hometown of band members Jimin and Jung Kook. All seven members of the band will use some of the hiatus time for military service, which is mandatory in South Korea.

SIGNING SENSATION
THREE MILLION VIEWS FOR *ENCANTO* SIGN LANGUAGE VIDEO

The breakout song of *Encanto*, "We Don't Talk About Bruno," spurred many covers. One of the biggest translated the song into British Sign Language! Disney worked with Deaf Talent Collective in the UK to create a music video using BSL to celebrate the International Day of Sign Languages in September. The video had more than 3 million viewers watching Deaf Talent perform on YouTube.

TAYLOR VS TICKETMASTER
FURY OVER TICKET SALES FIASCO

Taylor Swift announced her first tour in five years, the "Eras Tour," in November 2022. But when ticket sales opened, the hosting site, Ticketmaster, was unable to cope with the huge demand; the site crashed, leaving fans in a virtual line, and Ticketmaster then canceled remaining ticket sales, prompting outrage. Swift criticized Ticketmaster on Instagram and now the US Senate has asked the Justice Department to investigate the site's stranglehold on the industry.

MUSIC MAKERS

MOST-STREAMED SONG OF 2022
"AS IT WAS"
HARRY STYLES

MOST-STREAMED SONGS OF 2022
1. Harry Styles, "As It Was"
2. Glass Animals, "Heat Waves"
3. The Kid LAROI with Justin Bieber, "STAY"
4. Bad Bunny and Chencho Corleone, "Me Porto Benito"
5. Bad Bunny, "Tití Me Preguntó"

With more than 1.5 billion plays on Spotify, the most-streamed song of 2022 was Harry Styles's smash hit "As It Was." The song, which is the first single from the singer's third solo album, *Harry's House*, also broke the record for most-streamed song in a twenty-four-hour period—it was played more than 16 million times on April 1, the day it was released—and broke the record for most streams in a week, with 78,460,903 by April 8. It's no surprise that *Harry's House* itself came in as Spotify's second-most-streamed album of the year, after Bad Bunny's *Un Verano Sin Ti*. As well as his massive musical success, Styles had a big year on-screen in 2022, with two lead movie roles.

TOP-SELLING ALBUM OF 2022
MIDNIGHTS
TAYLOR SWIFT

The tenth studio album from pop sensation Taylor Swift, *Midnights*, sold six million copies worldwide to win the title of 2022's best-selling album. This number includes sales in all formats, including digital downloads, CDs, and vinyl. With *Midnights*, Swift topped the bestseller list for the third time in four years, after *Folklore* in 2020 and *Lover* in 2019. *Midnights* is also the highest-selling album since Swift's *Reputation* in 2017, generating around $230 million for her label, Universal, and accounting for an amazing 3 percent of its 2022 revenue. Scattered sleepless nights Swift experienced throughout her life shape the songs of *Midnights*, which was released at midnight on October 21, 2022.

MUSIC MAKERS

MOST-LIKED VIDEO ON YOUTUBE
"DESPACITO"

"Despacito" remains the most-liked video on YouTube, hitting 50 million likes in October 2022. The Puerto Rican dance track by Luis Fonsi, which features Daddy Yankee, came out in 2017 and took only six months to become the most-streamed song in history. It's no surprise that it also became the first music video to notch up four, five, six, and seven billion views on YouTube, before hitting eight billion in November 2022. That's not to say it's everybody's favorite. According to YouTube's stats, the video is also in the top 20 most-disliked videos on the channel, with more than five million dislikes before YouTube made them invisible.

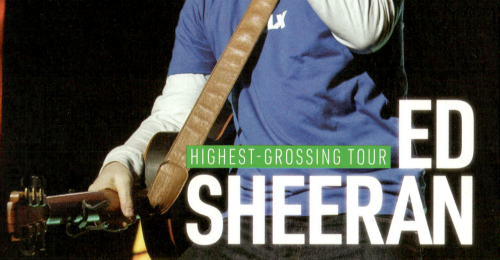

HIGHEST-GROSSING TOUR
ED SHEERAN

HIGHEST-GROSSING TOURS
Millions

- 776.2 — Ed Sheeran, ÷ (*Divide*)
- 750 — Elton John, Farewell Yellow Brick Road
- 736.4 — U2, 360°
- 584.2 — Guns N' Roses, Not in This Lifetime . . .
- 558.2 — The Rolling Stones, A Bigger Bang

British singer-songwriter Ed Sheeran has the highest-grossing tour of all time, surpassing those of Elton John, U2, Guns N' Roses, and the Rolling Stones. Sheeran's tour for his album ÷ (*Divide*) grossed $776.2 million, making it the biggest moneymaker ever for a musical tour. Sheeran's impressive title is no doubt helped by the fact that the tour stretched for longer than two years, beginning in Turin, Italy, in March 2017 and ending in Ipswich, England, in August 2019. By the time it was over, Sheeran had visited forty-three countries and had performed before more than 8.5 million people.

MUSIC MAKERS

DRAKE
FIRST RAPPER TO TOP *BILLBOARD* 100 CHART

Drake released his album *If You're Reading This It's Too Late* through iTunes on February 12, 2015. The digital album sold 495,000 units in its first week and entered the *Billboard* 100 at no. 1, making Drake the first rap artist ever to top the chart. The album also helped Drake secure another record: most hits on the *Billboard* 100 at one time. On March 7, 2015, Drake had fourteen hit songs on the chart, matching the record the Beatles have held since 1964. Since releasing his first hit single, "Best I Ever Had," in 2009, Drake has seen many of his singles go multiplatinum, including "Hotline Bling," which sold 41,000 copies in its first week and had eighteen weeks at no.1 on the *Billboard* 100.

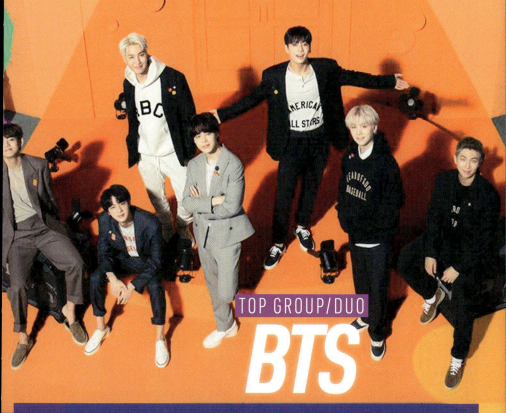

TOP GROUP/DUO
BTS

In 2022, K-pop royalty BTS were named top group at the *Billboard* Music Awards for the third year in a row, tying them with One Direction for most wins. Their wildly successful year included a Las Vegas residency, *Permission to Dance on Stage*, which earned them more than $35 million; a record-breaking fourth win for favorite pop group/duo at the American Music Awards; and even a visit to the White House to speak about anti-Asian hate crimes. The year 2022 also saw chart-topping collaborations for the septet, including "Bad Decisions" with Benny Blanco and Snoop Dogg; Jung Kook's "Left and Right" with Charlie Puth; and Jin's solo debut, "The Astronaut," written with Coldplay.

MUSIC MAKERS

TOP-SELLING RECORDING GROUP
THE BEATLES

The Beatles continue to hold the record for best-selling recording group in the United States, with 183 million albums sold. The British band recorded their first album in September 1962 and made their *Billboard* debut with "I Want to Hold Your Hand." Before breaking up in 1969, the group had twenty number one songs and recorded some of the world's most famous albums, including *Sgt. Pepper's Lonely Hearts Club Band*.

TOP-SELLING RECORDING ARTISTS IN THE UNITED STATES
Albums sold in millions

- 183 The Beatles
- 157 Garth Brooks
- 146.5 Elvis Presley
- 120 Eagles
- 112.5 Led Zeppelin

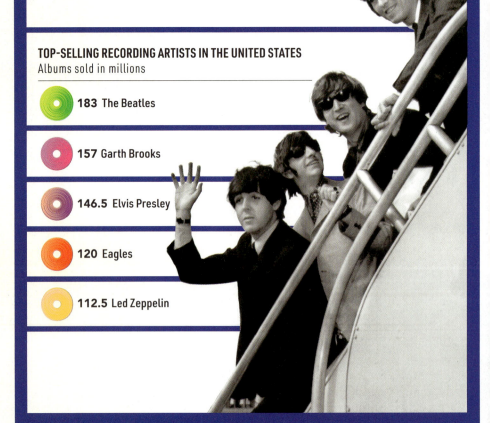

LONGEST-EVER MUSIC VIDEO
"LEVEL OF CONCERN" TWENTY ONE PILOTS

Twenty One Pilots collaborated with their fans in 2020 to create the longest music video ever! The official video for their hit "Level of Concern" lasted 177 days, 16 hours, 10 minutes, and 25 seconds, with the song constantly looping as fan-made video submissions were played on the live stream. The band announced the end of its "never-ending" stream by joking that the only way it would stop was for the power to go out . . . followed by a video of band member Joshua Dun overloading his Christmas tree with lights!

MUSIC MAKERS

RICHEST FEMALE SINGER
RIHANNA

Forbes officially named Robyn "Rihanna" Fenty a billionaire in 2022, certifying the Barbadian icon as the richest female singer in the world. Her estimated $1.7 billion net worth doesn't just come from her eight studio albums—$1.4 billion comes from her Fenty Beauty makeup line. With a diverse range of shades for all skin tones and a commitment to cruelty-free production, Rihanna's cosmetics line is a real hit, outshining many other celebrity contributions to the industry.

"OLD TOWN ROAD"

LONGEST-RUNNING NO. 1 SINGLE

From March through July 2019, rapper Lil Nas X's "Old Town Road" spent seventeen weeks in the no. 1 spot, pushing past "Despacito" from Luis Fonsi and Mariah Carey's "One Sweet Day," each of which spent sixteen weeks at the top of the charts. Lil Nas X's real name is Montero Hill, and he is from Atlanta, Georgia. He recorded the song himself, and people first fell in love with the catchy tune on TikTok. "Old Town Road" made it to the country charts, but it was later dropped for not being considered a country song. Disagreements about its genre only fueled interest in the song, however, and it subsequently hit no. 1. The song was then remixed and rerecorded with country music star Billy Ray Cyrus, whose wife at the time, Tish, encouraged him to become involved.

MUSIC MAKERS

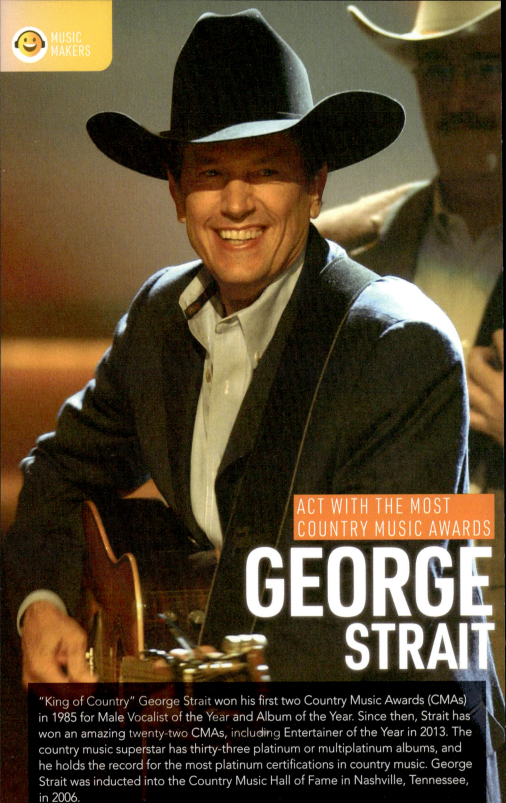

ACT WITH THE MOST COUNTRY MUSIC AWARDS

GEORGE STRAIT

"King of Country" George Strait won his first two Country Music Awards (CMAs) in 1985 for Male Vocalist of the Year and Album of the Year. Since then, Strait has won an amazing twenty-two CMAs, including Entertainer of the Year in 2013. The country music superstar has thirty-three platinum or multiplatinum albums, and he holds the record for the most platinum certifications in country music. George Strait was inducted into the Country Music Hall of Fame in Nashville, Tennessee, in 2006.

MUSICIAN WITH THE MOST GRAMMYS

BEYONCÉ

Queen Bey reigned supreme in 2023, becoming the musician with the most Grammys of all time after four wins at the 65th Grammy Awards ceremony. Her seventh studio album, *Renaissance*, won Best Dance/Electronic Album; while songs from the album won Best R&B Song ("Cuff It"); Best Traditional R&B Vocal Performance ("Plastic Off the Sofa"); and Best Dance Recording ("Break My Soul") to bring her total wins to thirty-two. Both Beyoncé and her husband, Jay-Z, have eighty-eight Grammy nominations, tying them for most-nominated artists of all time.

MUSIC MAKERS

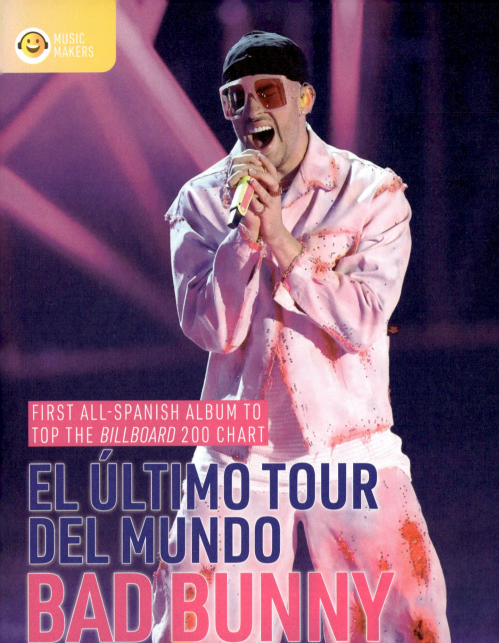

FIRST ALL-SPANISH ALBUM TO TOP THE *BILLBOARD* 200 CHART

EL ÚLTIMO TOUR DEL MUNDO
BAD BUNNY

Bad Bunny's debut album *El Último Tour del Mundo* (*The Last Tour in the World*) made music history in 2020, landing the top spot on *Billboard*'s 200 album chart. It's the first time in *Billboard*'s sixty-four-year history that an album performed entirely in Spanish has reached no. 1. The album, featuring a mix of Latin trap, reggaeton, and ska-punk, was one of three albums released by the Puerto Rican rapper, singer, and songwriter in 2020. His second album, *YHLQMDLG*, made it as high as no. 2 on the chart in March. Bad Bunny, whose birth name is Benito Martínez Ocasio, ended 2020 as Spotify's most-streamed artist of the year, amassing a staggering 8.3 billion streams.

MOST-AWARDED ARTIST
TAYLOR SWIFT

Taylor Swift beat her own record again in 2022! With six more wins at the American Music Awards, she brought her total number to forty. She remains the ceremony's most-awarded artist of all time. At the 2022 AMAs, Swift won Artist of the Year, Favorite Country Album, Favorite Pop Album, and Favorite Music Video for her rereleased album *Red (Taylor's Version)*. She also took home Favorite Female Pop Artist and Favorite Female Country Artist. This puts Swift way ahead of the next most-awarded artist, Michael Jackson, with twenty-four. With the release of her new album, *Midnights*, in 2022 and more re-releases on the horizon, it seems inevitable that Swift will continue to widen that gap for some time.

CHAPTER 2
SCREEN & STAGE

SCREEN & STAGE
TRENDING

WICKED MOVES
NETFLIX'S *WEDNESDAY*'S DANCE SCENE

Wednesday was Netflix's biggest new show of 2022, breaking records for the most hours viewed in a week on the platform. Fans loved Jenna Ortega's take on title character Wednesday Addams, but one scene in particular sparked a new musical trend. Ortega's spooky choreography to "Goo Goo Muck" by the Cramps was adapted into a viral TikTok dance using a sped-up version of Lady Gaga's "Bloody Mary."

SHOWSTOPPER
KIM K. WEARS MARILYN MONROE'S DRESS

Kim Kardashian made—and wore—fashion history at the 2022 Met Gala when she arrived wearing a dress once belonging to Marilyn Monroe. The dress, worn by Monroe in 1962 when she sang "Happy Birthday" to President John F. Kennedy, was loaned out by Ripley's Believe It or Not! museum. While Kardashian wore the dress only for the red carpet before changing into a replica, it sparked outrage among those who accused Kardashian of damaging the fragile historical piece.

INSPIRED CASTING
KIDS REACT TO HALLE BAILEY'S ARIEL

When the trailer for Disney's *The Little Mermaid* dropped in 2022, African American actress Halle Bailey's casting as Ariel was particularly inspiring to little Black girls. It kick-started a new TikTok trend among parents watching their children react to the first reveal of Bailey's face. Many of these videos went viral as they captured the joy of young Black viewers who saw a mermaid who looked just like them.

SUPER SPICY!
MILLIE BOBBY BROWN TAKES THE HOT WING CHALLENGE

Stranger Things star Millie Bobby Brown went viral during the season four press tour after going on *Hot Ones*—a talk show in which host Sean Evans asks guests questions as they eat progressively spicier chicken wings. Brown couldn't handle the heat, and her reaction to trying to eat one had the whole Internet in stitches as she realized her mistake and began desperately chugging her chocolate milkshake.

"MY MONEY DON'T JIGGLE JIGGLE"
LOUIS THEROUX BECOMES A TIKTOK MEME

One of the best sounds on TikTok in 2022 was "My Money Don't Jiggle Jiggle," a song created with a sample of Louis Theroux rapping on Amelia Dimoldenberg's *Chicken Shop Date* series. Producers Duke & Jones turned the clip into a song in less than fifteen minutes, little knowing that it would become TikTok's eighth-most played song of 2022.

25

STAGE & SCREEN

LONGEST-RUNNING SCRIPTED
TV SHOW IN THE UNITED STATES

THE SIMPSONS

The Simpsons entered its thirty-fourth season in 2022, continuing to break its own record as the longest-running American sitcom, cartoon, and scripted prime-time television show in history. The animated comedy, which first aired in December 1989, centers on the antics and everyday lives of the Simpson family. Famous guest stars who have made appearances over the years range from Stephen Hawking to Kelsey Grammer and Ed Sheeran (as Lisa's new crush). Fox has renewed the show for the upcoming thirty-fifth and thirty-sixth seasons, too.

CHILDREN'S/FAMILY SHOW WITH THE MOST EMMYS
HEARTSTOPPER

2022 was the first year that a separate awards show was held for the Children's & Family Emmys, celebrating the best of TV aimed at younger audiences. The 1st Annual Children's & Family Emmys, held in December and hosted by *Dance Moms*' Jojo Siwa, saw Netflix's *Heartstopper* win five awards to become the winningest show so far in the ceremony's history. Based on a hugely successful graphic novel series of the same name, *Heartstopper* won awards for Outstanding Young Teen Series and for Outstanding Casting, while its creator Alice Oseman won for Outstanding Writing. The show's stars also did well: Kit Connor won Outstanding Lead Performance for his role as romantic lead Nick Nelson, while Olivia Colman won the award for Outstanding Guest Actor for playing his mom.

STAGE & SCREEN

MOST POPULAR GAME SHOW
JEOPARDY!

Jeopardy!, which entered its thirty-ninth season in September 2022, remains the most popular game show on television with about 20 million viewers per week. The show's continuing success following the loss of its late host Alex Trebek led the network to renew *Jeopardy!* for another five seasons into 2027–2028, alongside sister show *Wheel of Fortune*. The new *Jeopardy!* cohosts, Ken Jennings and Mayim Bialik, oversaw some thrilling moments in 2022, including the end of fan favorite Amy Schneider's forty-game winning streak on January 27. Not only did Schneider win an epic total of $1,382,800 during her season thirty-eight run, but the Ohio native and former software engineer also won the $250,000 prize in the Tournament of Champions in November.

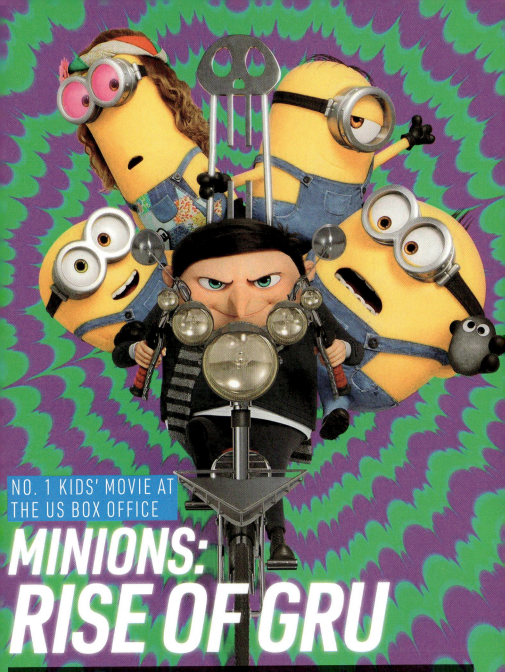

NO. 1 KIDS' MOVIE AT THE US BOX OFFICE

MINIONS: RISE OF GRU

Grossing $370 million at the US box office, Universal Studios' *Minions: The Rise of Gru* was the number one kids' movie in 2022. Set in the 1970s, the story follows twelve-year-old Gru, who is determined to establish himself as a master of evil. Aided by minions Kevin, Stuart, Bob, and Otto, he takes on supervillain supergroup the Vicious 6. Naturally, he outsmarts them at every turn. More than a decade after the release of *Despicable Me* (2010), the success of *Minions: The Rise of Gru* shows that the appeal of the supervillain, played by Steve Carell, and his lovable yellow friends is far from diminishing.

STAGE & SCREEN

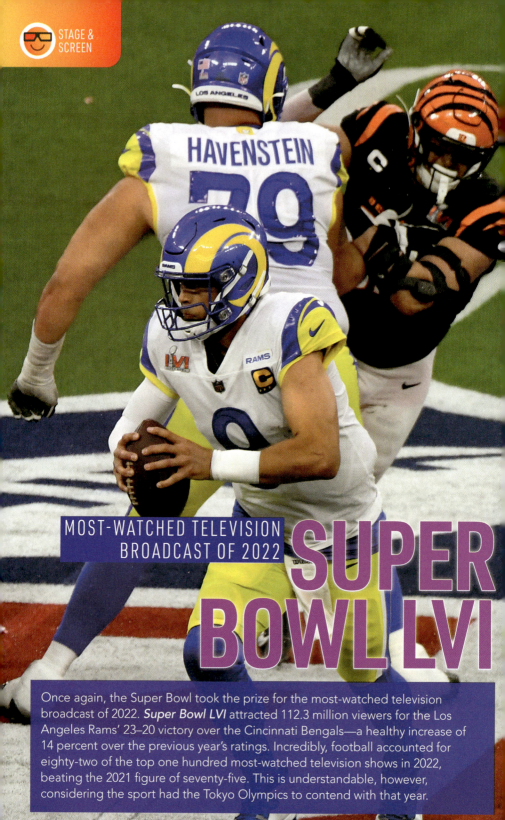

MOST-WATCHED TELEVISION BROADCAST OF 2022

SUPER BOWL LVI

Once again, the Super Bowl took the prize for the most-watched television broadcast of 2022. *Super Bowl LVI* attracted 112.3 million viewers for the Los Angeles Rams' 23–20 victory over the Cincinnati Bengals—a healthy increase of 14 percent over the previous year's ratings. Incredibly, football accounted for eighty-two of the top one hundred most-watched television shows in 2022, beating the 2021 figure of seventy-five. This is understandable, however, considering the sport had the Tokyo Olympics to contend with that year.

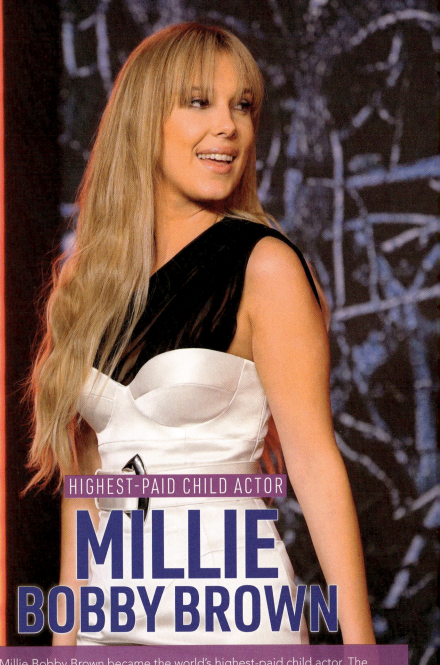

HIGHEST-PAID CHILD ACTOR
MILLIE BOBBY BROWN

In 2019, Millie Bobby Brown became the world's highest-paid child actor. The British actress earned $350,000 for every episode of *Stranger Things* season three, putting her on a level with her adult costars. Her net worth was estimated to be $14 million in November 2022. The actress earned $10 million for reprising her role as the young detective in *Enola Holmes 2*, the highest salary ever for an actor under the age of twenty. As well as acting, Brown earns money through modeling work and various brand endorsements, but she makes sure to use her wealth for good! Brown is a UNICEF Goodwill Ambassador and has also raised money for the Olivia Hope Foundation with her makeup line, florence by mills.

STAGE & SCREEN

MARVEL CINEMATIC UNIVERSE

MOST SUCCESSFUL MOVIE FRANCHISE

MOST SUCCESSFUL MOVIE FRANCHISES
Total worldwide gross, in billions of US dollars (as of January 2023)

Franchise	Gross
Marvel Cinematic Universe	27.9
Star Wars	10.3
Spider-Man	9.8
Harry Potter	9.7
James Bond	7.8

The Marvel Cinematic Universe franchise has grossed more than $27.9 billion worldwide! This impressive total includes ticket sales from the huge hits of 2018, *Black Panther* and *Avengers: Infinity War*. *Black Panther* grossed $1.34 billion worldwide within three months of its release, but then *Avengers: Infinity War* hit the screens, taking in $1.82 billion worldwide in its first month. With *Avengers: Endgame* earning even greater revenues in 2019, as well as the successful launch of Marvel's Phase Four in 2021 and continued excitement for the franchise, the Marvel Cinematic Universe looks set to hold this record for the foreseeable future.

FIRST ASIAN WOMAN TO WIN BEST ACTRESS AT THE OSCARS

MICHELLE YEOH

Malaysian-born Michelle Yeoh made Oscar history at the 2023 Academy Awards, becoming the first Asian woman to win the award for Best Actress. Yeoh won the Oscar for her role in *Everything Everywhere All at Once*, in which she plays a middle-aged Chinese American laundromat owner who gains superpowers and experiences different lives in multiple parallel universes. The adventure-packed film is at once funny and charming, with sixty-year-old Yeoh performing most of her own stunts. At the awards, Yeoh accepted her Oscar with an emotional speech that included the words: "For all the little boys and girls who look like me watching tonight, this is proof that dreams do come true."

STAGE & SCREEN

YOUNGEST ACTRESS NOMINATED FOR AN OSCAR

QUVENZHANÉ WALLIS

At nine years old, Quvenzhané Wallis became the youngest-ever Academy Award nominee for Best Actress. She received the nomination in 2013 for her role as Hushpuppy in *Beasts of the Southern Wild*. Although Wallis did not win the Oscar, she went on to gain forty-one more nominations and win twenty-four acting honors at various industry awards shows.
In 2015, she received a Golden Globe Best Actress nomination for her role in *Annie*. Wallis was five years old when she auditioned for Hushpuppy, and she won the part over four thousand other candidates.

YOUNGEST ACTOR NOMINATED FOR AN OSCAR
JUSTIN HENRY

Justin Henry was just eight years old when he received a Best Supporting Actor nomination in 1980 for a role he played at age seven. His neighbor, a casting director, suggested that Henry try out for the part. Although the young actor lost out on the Oscar, *Kramer vs. Kramer* won several, including Best Actor for Dustin Hoffman, Best Actress in a Supporting Role for Meryl Streep, and Best Picture. Justin Henry appeared in a few other films before leaving acting to finish his education. He returned to acting in the 1990s.

STAGE & SCREEN

TOP-EARNING KID YOUTUBER
RYAN KAJI

Ryan Kaji, the star of *Ryan's World*, made $29.5 million in 2022 as the highest-earning kid on YouTube at eleven years old. *Ryan's World* has attracted more than 34 million subscribers, with the number set to keep on growing. In 2017, Kaji became the youngest-ever person on a Forbes top-earners list when his channel made $11 million. At the time, he was just six years old! His content has changed since then, from reviewing toys to posting educational videos about his interests in the sciences, arts and crafts, and music. Videos on *Ryan's World* also feature his parents and his younger sisters, twins Emma and Kate.

MOST POPULAR YOUTUBE CHANNEL
COCOMELON

The preschoolers are taking over! *CoComelon Nursery Rhymes*, a channel with colorful animated nursery rhymes, became the most-viewed YouTube channel in the United States in 2021 and the top global channel in English. Originally started as a hobby by two parents in Orange County, California, the popular channel ended 2021 with 828.8 million weekly views, 126 million subscribers, and earnings of over $100 million for the year. The channel's most-watched video, "Bath Song," was uploaded in May 2018 and had 6.1 billion views as of April 2023 . . . that's a lot of baths!

STAGE & SCREEN

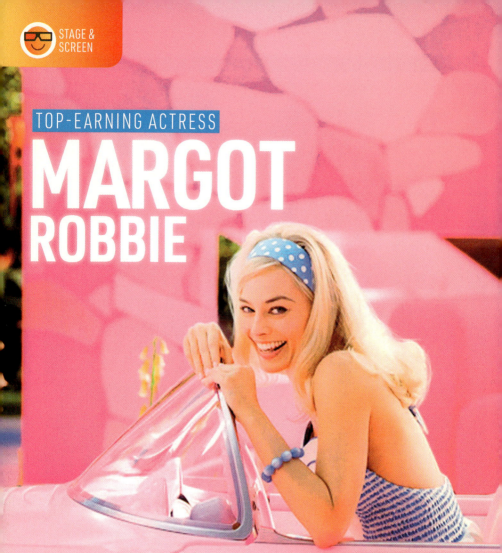

TOP-EARNING ACTRESS
MARGOT ROBBIE

Margot Robbie made $12.5 million in 2022 for playing *Barbie* in director Greta Gerwig's take on the famous doll. This salary was not only the highest per-film salary an actress made in 2022, but also notable for being equal to what her male costar, Ryan Gosling, earned for playing Ken. While this impressive payday put Robbie on the top-ten list for highest-earning movie stars of all genders that year, she still made $87.5 million less than the top-earning actor (Tom Cruise, for *Maverick*). In better news, several other actresses hit the $10 million per-film threshold for films in production in 2022, including Sandra Bullock for *The Lost City,* Zendaya for *Challengers*, Lady Gaga for *Joker 2*, and Millie Bobby Brown for *Enola Holmes 2*.

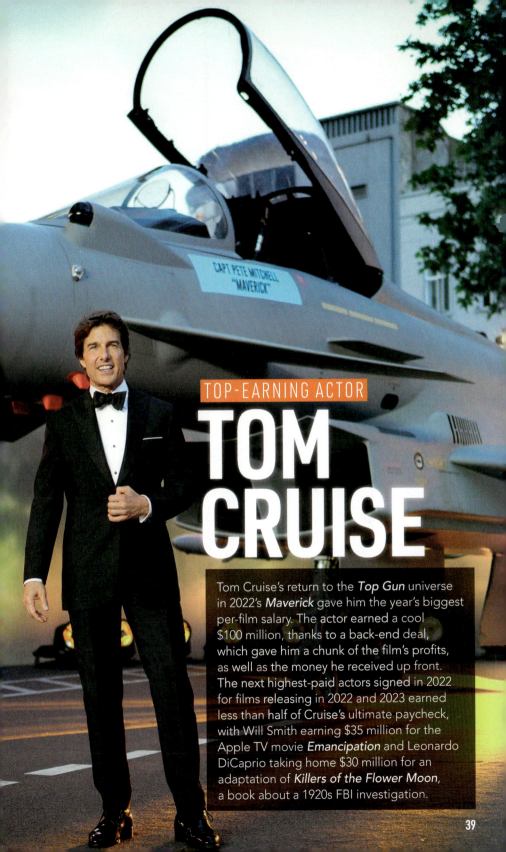

TOP-EARNING ACTOR
TOM CRUISE

Tom Cruise's return to the *Top Gun* universe in 2022's *Maverick* gave him the year's biggest per-film salary. The actor earned a cool $100 million, thanks to a back-end deal, which gave him a chunk of the film's profits, as well as the money he received up front. The next highest-paid actors signed in 2022 for films releasing in 2022 and 2023 earned less than half of Cruise's ultimate paycheck, with Will Smith earning $35 million for the Apple TV movie *Emancipation* and Leonardo DiCaprio taking home $30 million for an adaptation of *Killers of the Flower Moon*, a book about a 1920s FBI investigation.

STAGE & SCREEN

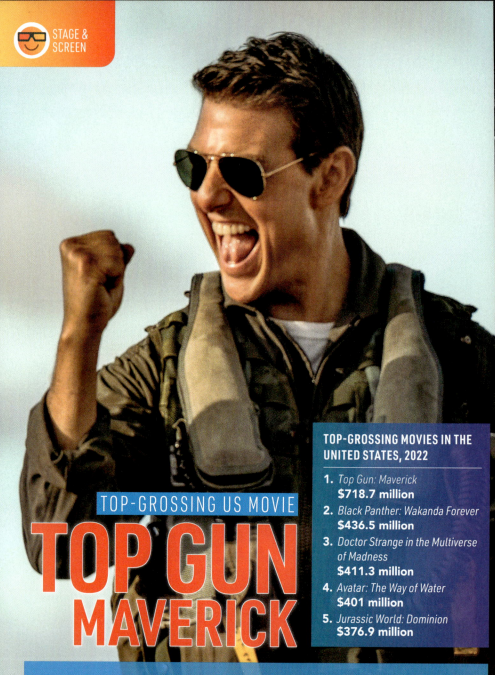

TOP-GROSSING US MOVIE

TOP GUN MAVERICK

TOP-GROSSING MOVIES IN THE UNITED STATES, 2022

1. *Top Gun: Maverick*
   $718.7 million
2. *Black Panther: Wakanda Forever*
   $436.5 million
3. *Doctor Strange in the Multiverse of Madness*
   $411.3 million
4. *Avatar: The Way of Water*
   $401 million
5. *Jurassic World: Dominion*
   $376.9 million

Top Gun: Maverick was the highest-grossing film at the US box office in 2022, holding the no. 1 spot on both Memorial Day and Labor Day. *Maverick* is the only film ever to have done so. At the end of 2022, the film had made $718.7 million, displacing Marvel's *Black Panther* as the fifth-highest-grossing film ever in the United States. Internationally, however, *Maverick* was beaten by James Cameron's massive *Avatar* sequel, *The Way of Water*, which hit $1.9 billion worldwide compared to *Maverick*'s $1.4 billion. Both movies are long-awaited follow-ups to high-earning original films.

TOP-GROSSING ANIMATED-FILM FRANCHISE

DESPICABLE ME

Following the 2022 release of *Minions: The Rise of Gru*, and with a global total of $4.64 billion, *Despicable Me* remains the world's highest-grossing animated franchise of all time. The 2015 spin-off, *Minions*, is the most profitable animated film in Universal Studios' history and was the highest-grossing film of the year, while *Despicable Me 3* and Oscar-nominated *Despicable Me 2* hit spot no. 2 in their respective years of release. Collectively, the four movies beat the *Shrek* franchise's earnings of $3.55 billion. In 2019, *Frozen II* became the biggest-selling animated movie ever with earnings of $1.45 billion worldwide.

STAGE & SCREEN

LONGEST-RUNNING BROADWAY SHOW
THE PHANTOM OF THE OPERA

LONGEST-RUNNING BROADWAY SHOWS
Total performances (as of April 2023)

The Phantom of the Opera	13,981
Chicago (1996 revival)	10,337
The Lion King	9,953
Wicked	7,493
Cats	7,485

Marking the end of an impressive thirty-five years on Broadway, the cast of Andrew Lloyd Webber's *The Phantom of the Opera* made its last appearance on April 16, 2023. The show has been performed 13,981 times, making it the longest-running Broadway show ever. The story, based on a novel written in 1911 by French author Gaston Leroux, tells the tragic tale of the phantom and his love for an opera singer, Christine.

THE LION KING

HIGHEST-GROSSING BROADWAY MUSICAL

Since opening on November 13, 1997, *The Lion King* has earned more than $1.7 billion. It's Broadway's third-longest-running production and is an adaptation of the hugely popular Disney animated film. Along with hit songs from the movie such as "Circle of Life" and "Hakuna Matata," the show includes new compositions by South African composer Lebo M. and others. The Broadway show features songs in six African languages, including Swahili and Congolese. Since it opened, *The Lion King* has attracted audiences totaling over one hundred million people.

STAGE & SCREEN

HAMILTON
MUSICAL WITH THE MOST TONY AWARD NOMINATIONS

Lin-Manuel Miranda's musical biography of Founding Father Alexander Hamilton racked up sixteen Tony Award nominations to unseat the previous record holders, *The Producers* and *Billy Elliot: The Musical*, both of which had fifteen. The megahit hip-hop musical, which was inspired by historian Ron Chernow's biography of the first secretary of the treasury, portrays the Founding Fathers of the United States engaging in rap battles over issues such as the national debt and the French Revolution. *Hamilton* won eleven Tonys at the 2016 ceremony—one shy of *The Producers*, which retains the record for most Tony wins with twelve. *Hamilton*'s Broadway success paved the way for the show to open in Chicago in 2016, with a touring show and a London production following in 2017.

YOUNGEST WINNER OF A LAURENCE OLIVIER AWARD

ELEANOR WORTHINGTON-COX
CLEO DEMETRIOU
KERRY INGRAM
SOPHIA KIELY

In 2012, four actresses shared an Olivier Award for their roles in the British production of *Matilda*. Eleanor Worthington-Cox, Cleo Demetriou, Kerry Ingram, and Sophia Kiely all won the award for Best Actress in a Musical. Of the four actresses, Worthington-Cox, age ten, was the youngest by a few weeks. Each actress portraying *Matilda* performs two shows a week. In the United States, the four *Matilda* actresses won a special Tony Honors for Excellence in the Theatre in 2013. *Matilda*, inspired by the book by Roald Dahl, won a record seven Olivier Awards in 2012.

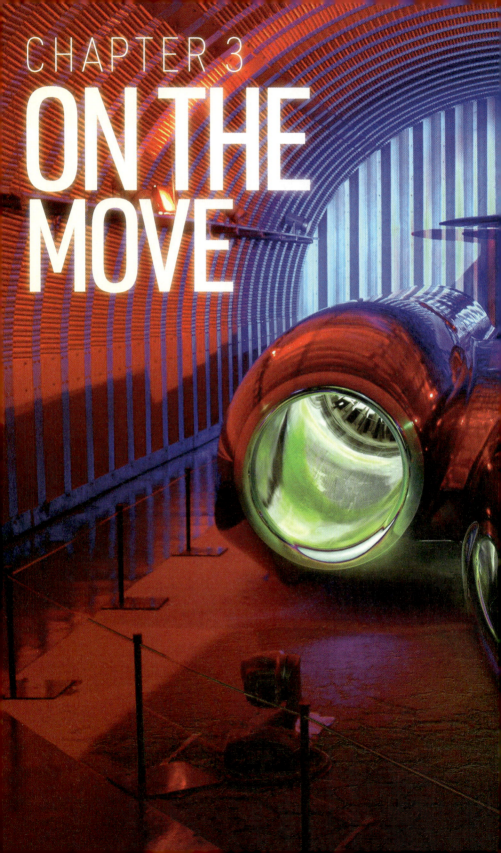

CHAPTER 3
ON THE MOVE

ON THE MOVE
TRENDING

CHOO CHOO!
WORLD'S LONGEST TRAIN

In 2022, the Rhaetian Railway company's 1.2-mile-long train set a new record for the world's longest passenger train as it celebrated the 175th anniversary of Switzerland's first railway. The train consisted of 25 "Capricorn" electric trains, with 100 cars between them, and required seven drivers and twenty-one technicians to guide it on its ceremonial journey through the Alps.

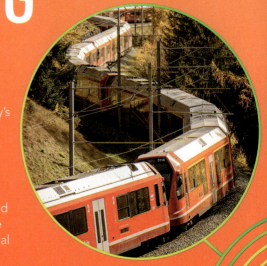

YACHT OF THE FUTURE
ZERO-EMISSION TRIMARAN CONCEPT REVEALED

Domus, a concept unveiled in 2022 by Rob Doyle Design and Van Geest Design, could be the first yacht over 750 gross tons to produce zero carbon dioxide emissions. This would be achieved through a combination of solar power, hydropower, and hydrogen fuel cells. The collaborative project is a 130-foot-long trimaran—a yacht with three hulls—that gets its name from a type of ancient Roman house built around an atrium. According to Doyle and Van Geest, their motto throughout the project was "Why not?"

EMERGENCY LANDING
PASSENGERS SAVE THE DAY

In May 2022, a Florida man with no prior piloting experience made the news for landing an airplane. Darren Harrison was a passenger on a small Cessna 208 when the pilot had a medical emergency. Harrison went into the cockpit, called air traffic control, and was coached through the flight and landing by Air Traffic Controller Robert Morgan. Thanks to his help and Harrison's quick thinking, the aircraft touched down safely at Palm Beach International Airport.

WE HAVE LIFTOFF!
FIRST ALL-PRIVATE TOURISM SPACE MISSION

Texas-based space tourism company Axiom Space launched its first all-private mission in April 2022. Axiom Mission 1 carried one flight commander and three paying passengers to the International Space Station using spacecraft from SpaceX. The SpaceX Dragon was launched from NASA's Kennedy Space Center in Florida. The tickets reportedly cost $55 million each, making space tourism accessible only to the richest travelers for now.

THE FUTURE IS NOW
ELECTRIC CAR'S SUCCESSFUL TEST FLIGHT

Soon drivers may be able to avoid traffic jams on the road by taking an unusual route—through the skies! Chinese company XPeng's electric taxi completed its first successful flight in 2022. The vehicle is a two-seater electric vertical takeoff and landing (eVTOL) aircraft that can achieve speeds up to 80 mph and does not produce carbon dioxide. The first flight of the XPeng X2 Electric Flying Car took place at Skydive Dubai in October, signaling the future of transportation has finally arrived.

ON THE MOVE

WORLD'S FIRST
MONSTER SCHOOL BUS

Bad to the Bone was the first monster school bus in the world. This revamped 1956 yellow bus is 13 feet tall, thanks to massive tires with 25-inch rims. The oversize bus weighs 19,000 pounds and is a favorite ride at charity events in California. But don't expect to get anywhere in a hurry—this "Kool Bus" is not built for speed and goes a maximum of just 7 miles per hour.

MOST EXPENSIVE MODERN STREET-LEGAL CAR
BOAT TAIL

For the second year running, and with an impressive price tag of $28 million, the stunning Rolls-Royce Boat Tail is the world's most expensive street-legal car. Three of these cars are being made for one private customer, each built to order by the manufacturer's custom Coachbuild division. With a sleek design inspired by luxury yachts of the early twentieth century, the convertible grand-touring car has a trunk that opens like a pair of butterfly wings to reveal luxury picnicking accessories that include a fridge stocked with the finest champagne!

MOST EXPENSIVE MODERN STREET-LEGAL CARS
In millions of US dollars

- $28 — Rolls-Royce Boat Tail
- $18.7 — Bugatti La Voiture Noire
- $17.6 — Pagani Zonda HP Barchetta
- $14.4 — SP Automotive Chaos
- $13 — Rolls-Royce Sweptail

ON THE MOVE

WORLD'S LONGEST MONSTER TRUCK

SIN CITY HUSTLER

Measuring a whopping 32 feet in length, standing 12 feet tall, and weighing 15,000 pounds, the Sin City Hustler is the world's longest monster truck. To put that into perspective, its measurements rival those of a *Tyrannosaurus rex*! The truck was custom-built by Brad and Jen Campbell of Big Toyz Racing in White Hills, Arizona, and currently resides in Las Vegas, Nevada. There, it is used as a tourist attraction. Twelve passengers can climb on board for the wildest drive of their lives!

QTvan

WORLD'S SMALLEST TRAILER

The tiny QTvan is just over 7 feet long, 2.5 feet wide, and 5 feet tall. Inside, however, it has a full-size single bed, a kettle for boiling water, and a 19-inch TV. The Environmental Transport Association (ETA) in Britain sponsored the invention of the minitrailer, which was designed to be pulled by a mobility scooter. The ETA recommends the QTvan for short trips only, since mobility scooters have a top speed of 6 miles per hour, at best.

ON THE MOVE

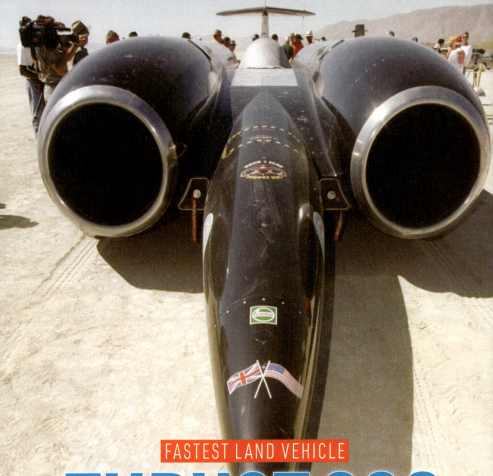

FASTEST LAND VEHICLE
THRUST SSC

The world's fastest car is the Thrust SSC, which reached a speed of 763 miles per hour on October 15, 1997, in the Black Rock Desert of Nevada. **SSC** stands for supersonic (faster than the speed of sound). The Thrust SSC's amazing speed comes from two jet engines with 110,000 brake horsepower. That's as much as 145 Formula One race cars. The British-made car uses about 5 gallons of jet fuel in one second and takes just five seconds to reach its top speed. At that speed, the Thrust SSC could travel from New York City to San Francisco in less than four hours. More recently, another British manufacturer has developed a new supersonic car, the Bloodhound, with a projected speed of 1,000 miles per hour. If it reaches that, it will set a new world record.

FASTEST PASSENGER TRAIN
SHANGHAI MAGLEV

The Shanghai Maglev, which runs between Shanghai Pudong International Airport and the outskirts of Shanghai, is currently the fastest passenger train in the world. The service reaches speeds of 268 miles per hour, covering the 19-mile distance in seven minutes and twenty seconds. *Maglev* is short for magnetic levitation, as the train moves by floating on magnets rather than with wheels on a track. Other high-speed trains, such as Japan's SCMaglev, may have reached higher speeds in testing (375 miles per hour), but are capped at 200 miles per hour when carrying passengers.

FASTEST PASSENGER TRAINS
(by maximum operating speed)

China **Shanghai Maglev**	268 mph
China **CR400 Fuxing**	217 mph
Germany **ICE3**	205 mph
France **TGV**	200 mph
Japan **JR East E5**	200 mph

 ON THE MOVE

FASTEST UNPILOTED PLANE X-43A

In November 2004, NASA launched its experimental X-43A plane for a test flight over the Pacific Ocean. The X-43A plane reached Mach 9.6, which is more than nine times the speed of sound and nearly 7,000 miles per hour. A B-52 aircraft carried the X-43A and a Pegasus rocket booster into the air, releasing them at 40,000 feet. At that point, the booster—essentially a fuel-packed engine—ignited, blasting the unpiloted X-43A higher and faster, before separating from the plane. The plane continued to fly for several minutes at 110,000 feet, before crashing (intentionally) into the ocean.

FASTEST HUMAN-MADE OBJECT

PARKER SOLAR PROBE

On November 21, 2021, and traveling at 364,621 miles per hour, the Parker Solar Probe set a new record for the fastest human-made object ever known. Jointly operated by NASA and Johns Hopkins University, and equipped with a wide range of scientific equipment, the Parker Solar Probe is on a seven-year mission to study the Sun's atmosphere. Withstanding extreme heat and radiation, it sends data and images back to Earth, revolutionizing our understanding of the star at the heart of our solar system. Also on November 21, 2021, the probe shattered a second record, having reached a distance of 5.3 million miles from the Sun's surface—the closest a spacecraft has ever been and less than one-tenth of the distance between the Sun and Earth.

FASTEST MANNED SPACECRAFT
APOLLO 10

NASA's Apollo 10 spacecraft reached its top speed on its descent to Earth, hurtling through the atmosphere at 24,816 miles per hour and splashing down on May 26, 1969. The spacecraft's crew had traveled faster than anyone on Earth. The mission was a "dress rehearsal" for the first moon landing by Apollo 11, two months later. The Apollo 10 spacecraft consisted of a Command and Service Module, called Charlie Brown, and a Lunar Module, called Snoopy. Today, Charlie Brown is on display at the Science Museum in London, England.

LIFTOFF
The Apollo 10 spacecraft was launched from Cape Canaveral, known as Cape Kennedy at the time. It was the fourth crewed Apollo launch in seven months.

APOLLO 10 FLIGHT STATS

05/18/1969 LAUNCH DATE

12:49 p.m. EDT LAUNCH

05/21/1969 DATE ENTERED LUNAR ORBIT

192:03:23 DURATION OF MISSION: 192 hours, 3 minutes, 23 seconds

05/26/1969 RETURN DATE

12:52 p.m. EDT SPLASHDOWN

ON THE MOVE

FASTEST ROLLER COASTER
FORMULA ROSSA

Thrill seekers hurtle along the Formula Rossa track at 149.1 miles per hour. The high-speed roller coaster is part of Ferrari World in Abu Dhabi, United Arab Emirates. Ferrari World also features the world's largest indoor theme park, at 1.5 million square feet. The Formula Rossa roller coaster seats are red Ferrari-shaped cars that travel from 0 to 62 miles per hour in just two seconds—as fast as a race car. The ride's G-force is so extreme that passengers must wear goggles to protect their eyes. G-force acts on a body due to acceleration and gravity. People can withstand 6 to 8 Gs for short periods. The Formula Rossa G-force is 4.8 Gs during acceleration and 1.7 Gs at maximum speed.

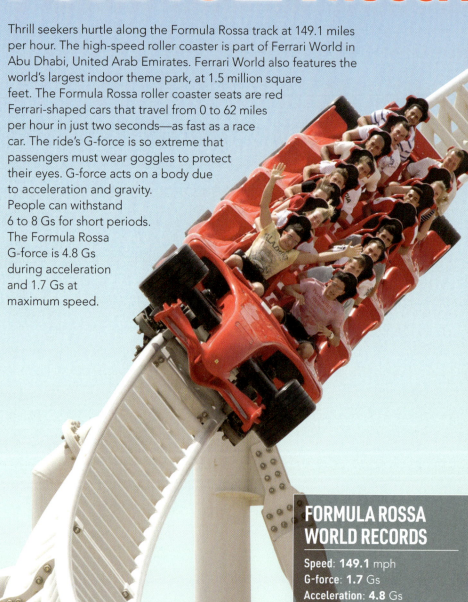

FORMULA ROSSA WORLD RECORDS

Speed: **149.1** mph
G-force: **1.7** Gs
Acceleration: **4.8** Gs

60

TALLEST WATER COASTER
TSUNAMI SURGE

Rising 86 feet above Hurricane Harbor Chicago amusement park, Tsunami Surge is the tallest water coaster in the world. Psychedelic visual effects light the way as thrill seekers are blasted through 950 feet of slides, tunnels, and hairpin bends at top speeds of 28 miles per hour. This attraction—the twenty-fifth to debut at the Six Flags park—uses the latest technology in jet propulsion to power its passengers all the way up the steepest slopes . . . and down again.

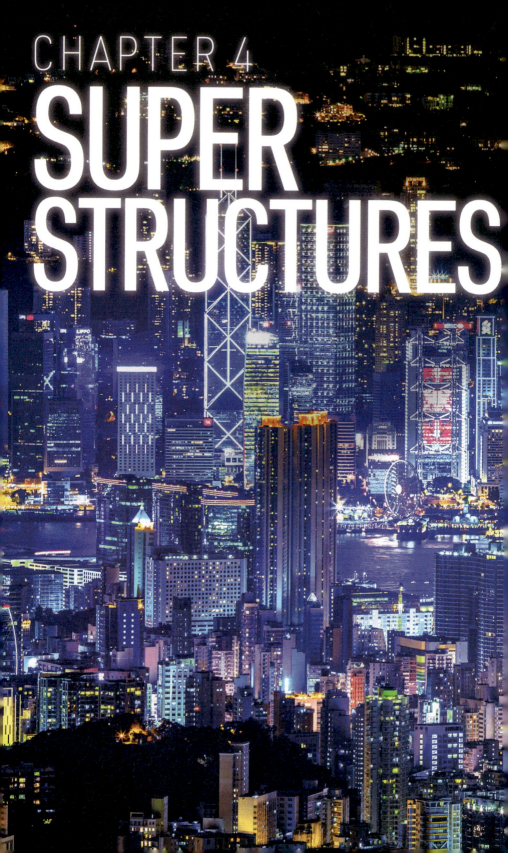

CHAPTER 4
SUPER STRUCTURES

SUPER STRUCTURES
TRENDING

COOL CONSTRUCTION
TEXAS HOUSE WITH 3D-PRINTED WALLS

Construction tech firm ICON is known for its work using 3D printing technology to build homes. In 2022, it collaborated with Lake|Flato Architecture to build House Zero, in East Austin, Texas, which has entirely 3D-printed walls. House Zero's walls are made from a material ICON calls Lavacrete and were printed in just ten days to create a 2,000-square-foot ranch house. The benefit of 3D printing is not only decreased production time, but also the reduction of the amount of waste from traditional construction methods.

PICTURE PERFECT
MOST INSTAGRAMMABLE HOTEL OF 2022

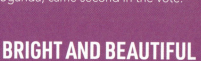

According to Luxury Travel Advisor, the Shore Club in Turks and Caicos was 2022's most Instagrammable place to stay, winning the vote for the second year in a row. The hotel's tagged Instagram pics show a paradise resort with its white beach, luxurious pools, and stunning views. Wildwaters Lodge on the Nile River, Uganda, came second in the vote.

BRIGHT AND BEAUTIFUL
SOLAR-POWERED ART GALLERY

Completed in 2022, Sydney Modern, part of the Art Gallery of New South Wales, is an awesome achievement in terms of sustainability: All its energy comes from renewable sources, including solar panels on the roof, a system to capture rainwater, and around 86,000 square feet of rooftop plants. Designed by Kazuyo Sejima and Ryue Nishizawa, it cost around $230 million.

SOLIDARITY
BUILDINGS LIGHT UP FOR UKRAINE

Russia's invasion of Ukraine in February 2022 led to an outpouring of support for Ukraine from around the world. While small businesses and families took to hanging Ukrainian flags in solidarity, many major buildings and monuments took it one step further by re-creating the flag with blue and yellow lights. Among the famous places to light up for Ukraine were the United States Capitol Building in Washington, DC; the Colosseum in Rome, Italy; and the Sydney Opera House in Australia.

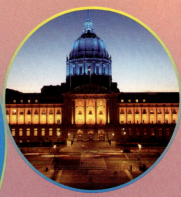

SUPER SKINNY
WORLD'S THINNEST SKYSCRAPER

Manhattan's "Billionaires' Row" is now home to a skyscraper that is 1,428 feet tall but only 58 feet wide, making it the world's skinniest skyscraper with a width-to-height slenderness ratio of 1:24. Because the new residential tower by SHoP Architects is built atop historic Steinway Hall at 111 West 57th Street, it has been dubbed "Steinway Tower" by some. However, the record-breaking building has its own issues: Some visitors have complained that the tower sways in high winds, and falling ice from the building injured passing drivers in February 2022.

SUPER STRUCTURES

CITY WITH THE MOST SKYSCRAPERS
HONG KONG

CITIES WITH THE MOST SKYSCRAPERS
Number of skyscrapers at 500 feet or higher

- Dubai, UAE
- New York City, US
- Shenzhen, China
- Hong Kong, China

Hong Kong, China, has 552 buildings that reach 500 feet or higher, six of which are actually 1,000 feet or higher. The tallest three are the International Commerce Centre (ICC) at 1,588 feet; Two International Finance Centre at 1,352 feet; and Central Plaza at 1,227 feet. Hong Kong's stunning skyline towers above Victoria Harbour. Most of its tallest buildings are on Hong Kong Island, although the other side of the harbor, Kowloon, is growing. Every night a light, laser, and sound show called "A Symphony of Lights" illuminates the sky against a backdrop of about forty of Hong Kong's skyscrapers.

WORLD'S LARGEST SPORTS STADIUM
RUNGRADO 1ST OF MAY STADIUM

It took over two years to build Rungrado 1st of May Stadium, a huge sports venue that has a capacity for up to 150,000 people. The 197-foot-tall stadium opened in 1989 on Rungra Island in North Korea's capital, Pyongyang. The stadium hosts international soccer matches on its natural grass pitch and has other facilities such as an indoor swimming pool, training halls, and a 1,312-foot rubberized running track. A newcomer to the list, the second-largest venue, India's Narendra Modi Stadium, was inaugurated in 2020.

LARGEST SPORTS STADIUMS
By capacity

Capacity	Stadium
150,000	**Rungrado 1st of May Stadium**, North Korea
132,000	**Narendra Modi Stadium**, Ahmedabad, India
107,601	**Michigan Stadium**, Michigan, US
106,572	**Beaver Stadium**, Pennsylvania, US
102,780	**Ohio Stadium**, Ohio, US

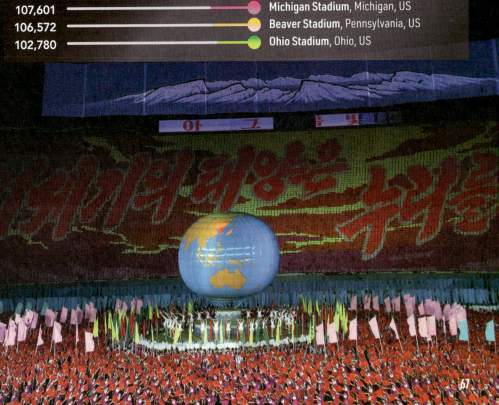

SUPER STRUCTURES

WORLD'S MOST EXPENSIVE HOTEL

LOVER'S DEEP

The spectacular *Lover's Deep*, a luxury submarine that spends the night touring the underwater world of St. Lucia in the Caribbean Sea, is currently the world's most expensive hotel. Attended by their own personal butler, guests sleep in spacious quarters full of extravagant furnishings, including a minibar area. As they sit back and relax, huge wraparound windows provide an ever-changing view of the colorful marine life outside. And the cost? Packages vary, but guests booking into the submarine can expect to spend a minimum of $150,000 for just one night.

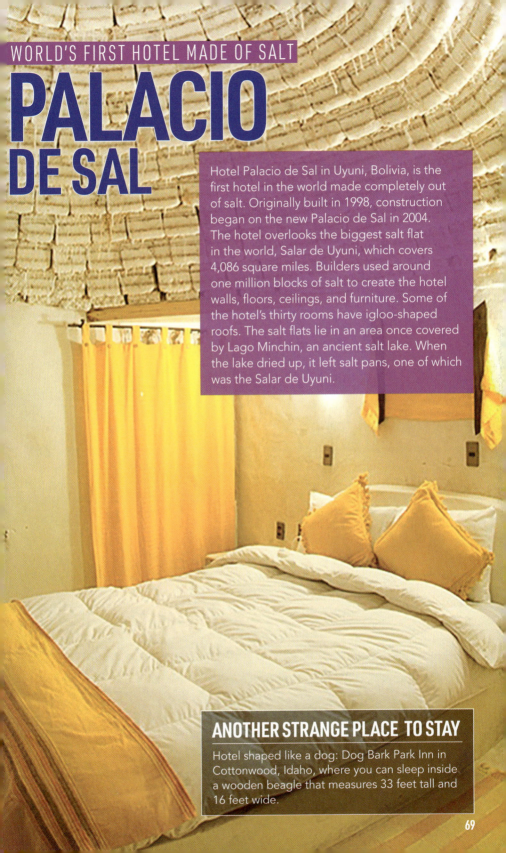

WORLD'S FIRST HOTEL MADE OF SALT
PALACIO DE SAL

Hotel Palacio de Sal in Uyuni, Bolivia, is the first hotel in the world made completely out of salt. Originally built in 1998, construction began on the new Palacio de Sal in 2004. The hotel overlooks the biggest salt flat in the world, Salar de Uyuni, which covers 4,086 square miles. Builders used around one million blocks of salt to create the hotel walls, floors, ceilings, and furniture. Some of the hotel's thirty rooms have igloo-shaped roofs. The salt flats lie in an area once covered by Lago Minchin, an ancient salt lake. When the lake dried up, it left salt pans, one of which was the Salar de Uyuni.

ANOTHER STRANGE PLACE TO STAY
Hotel shaped like a dog: Dog Bark Park Inn in Cottonwood, Idaho, where you can sleep inside a wooden beagle that measures 33 feet tall and 16 feet wide.

WORLD'S TALLEST BUILDING
BURJ KHALIFA

Holding the record for the world's tallest building since January 2010, the Burj Khalifa is 2,716.5 feet tall. It not only qualifies as the world's tallest building, but also the tallest human-made structure, the tallest freestanding structure, having the largest number of stories, and the highest aluminum and glass facades (which incidentally cover the same area as twenty-five football fields). The tower took six years to build, with 12,000 men on-site day after day, completing twenty-two million hours of work. Dubbed a "vertical city," the tower holds around 10,000 people at any given time.

DUBAI'S BURJ KHALIFA WORLD RECORDS:

1,654 FEET
Tallest elevator inside a building

163 FLOORS

1,448 FEET
Highest restaurant from ground level

TOUGH CLIMB
No fewer than 2,909 steps lead up to floor 160 of the Burj Khalifa. Anyone wishing to go higher has to do so climbing ladders.

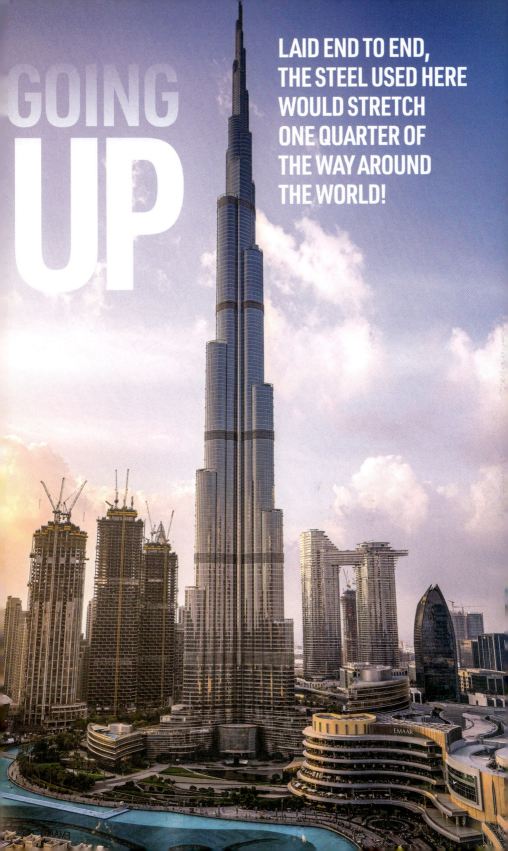

SUPER STRUCTURES

WORLD'S LARGEST FREESTANDING BUILDING

NEW CENTURY GLOBAL CENTER

The New Century Global Center in Chengdu, southwestern China, is a huge 18.9 million square feet. That's nearly three times the size of the Pentagon in Arlington, Virginia. Completed in 2013, the structure is 328 feet tall, 1,640 feet long, and 1,312 feet deep. The building houses a 4.3-million-square-foot shopping mall, two hotels, an Olympic-size ice rink, a fourteen-screen IMAX cinema complex, and offices. It even has its own Paradise Island, a beach resort complete with artificial sun.

WORLD'S LARGEST SWIMMING POOL
CITYSTARS POOL

Citystars Sharm El Sheikh lagoon in Egypt stretches over 29.7 acres. It was created by Crystal Lagoons, the same company that built the former record holder at San Alfonso del Mar in Chile. The lagoon at Sharm El Sheikh cost $5.5 million to create and is designed to be sustainable, using salt water from local underground aquifers. The creators purify this water not just for recreation, but also to provide clean, fresh water to the surrounding community.

LARGEST SWIMMING POOLS
Size in acres

Citystars Sharm El Sheikh, Egypt — 29.7
San Alfonso del Mar, Algarrobo, Chile — 19.8
MahaSamutr, Hua Hin, Thailand — 17.8
Ostrava Poruba, Czech Republic — 10.2
Diamante Cabo San Lucas, Mexico — 10.0

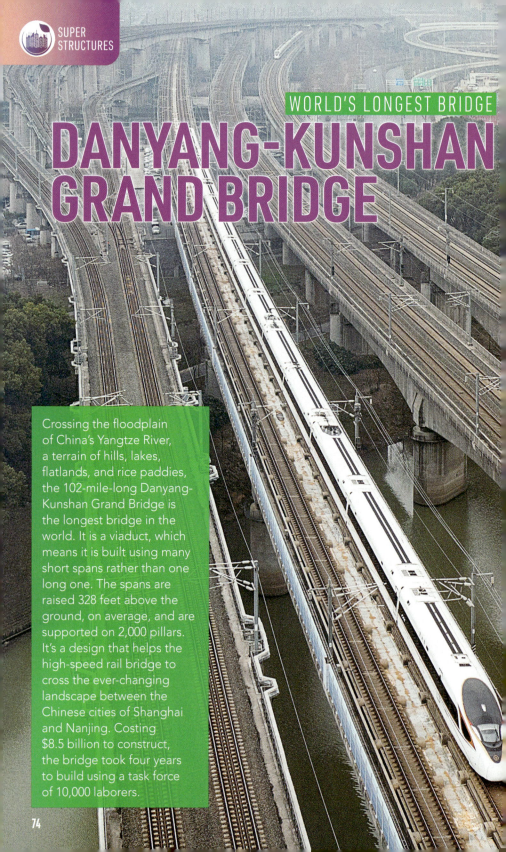

SUPER STRUCTURES

WORLD'S LONGEST BRIDGE
DANYANG-KUNSHAN GRAND BRIDGE

Crossing the floodplain of China's Yangtze River, a terrain of hills, lakes, flatlands, and rice paddies, the 102-mile-long Danyang-Kunshan Grand Bridge is the longest bridge in the world. It is a viaduct, which means it is built using many short spans rather than one long one. The spans are raised 328 feet above the ground, on average, and are supported on 2,000 pillars. It's a design that helps the high-speed rail bridge to cross the ever-changing landscape between the Chinese cities of Shanghai and Nanjing. Costing $8.5 billion to construct, the bridge took four years to build using a task force of 10,000 laborers.

WORLD'S MOST SUSTAINABLE CITY
OSLO

WORLD'S MOST SUSTAINABLE CITIES, 2022

OSLO · STOCKHOLM · TOKYO · COPENHAGEN · BERLIN

The most sustainable city in 2022 was Oslo, Norway's capital, according to the Arcadis Sustainable Cities Index. The index rates sustainability according to three criteria: Planet (environmental sustainability), People (social sustainability), and Profit (economic sustainability). Only two cities in the top ten were American, with Seattle, WA, coming in seventh and San Francisco, CA, at number nine. Oslo did particularly well in the Planet category due to its sustainable transport options, green spaces, and low levels of air pollution. This is no surprise, as Oslo is a key member of the Carbon Neutral Cities Alliance. Since 2016, the city has promised to reduce carbon emissions by 95 percent by 2030, and one of the ways it plans to do this is by reducing emissions from car traffic.

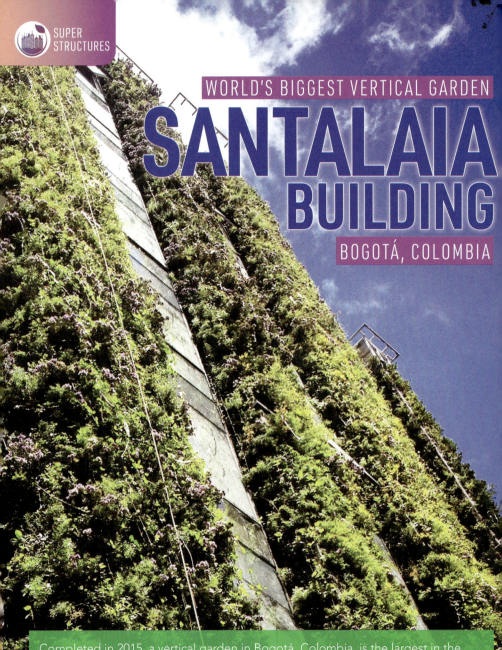

SUPER STRUCTURES

WORLD'S BIGGEST VERTICAL GARDEN
SANTALAIA BUILDING
BOGOTÁ, COLOMBIA

Completed in 2015, a vertical garden in Bogotá, Colombia, is the largest in the world. Known locally as the "green heart of Bogotá," the garden scales nine of the eleven stories of the Santalaia residential building in the Rosales neighborhood of the city and covers the facade in strips of green that alternate with the windows. Using a system developed by Spanish company Paisajismo Urbano, the green walls cover 33,551 square feet of garden in total—that's almost the size of twelve tennis courts. Beyond being beautiful, vertical gardens bring huge benefits to urban areas, filtering greenhouse gases, trapping dust particles, and helping to insulate the building, keeping rooms cool in summer, thereby reducing the need for energy-guzzling air-conditioning.

LARGEST-EVER SPACE TELESCOPE

JAMES WEBB SPACE TELESCOPE

Launched on December 25, 2021, the James Webb Space Telescope is the largest space telescope ever. While its forerunner, the Hubble Space Telescope, is roughly the size of a school bus, the Webb is more like the size of a tennis court. It is so big that it had to be folded up inside a rocket for launching. It was not until January 8, 2022, that the telescope's mirror fully unfolded for use, and it has now reached its destination some 930,000 miles away from Earth. The Webb is about one hundred times more powerful than its predecessor. Since July 12, 2022, NASA has released a number of spectacular color images captured by the telescope, revealing some of the earliest stars and galaxies in the universe.

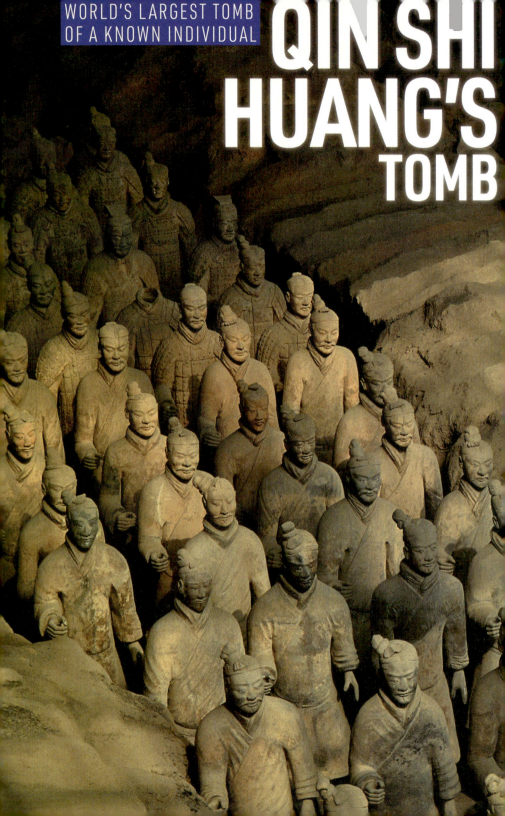

WORLD'S LARGEST TOMB OF A KNOWN INDIVIDUAL

QIN SHI HUANG'S TOMB

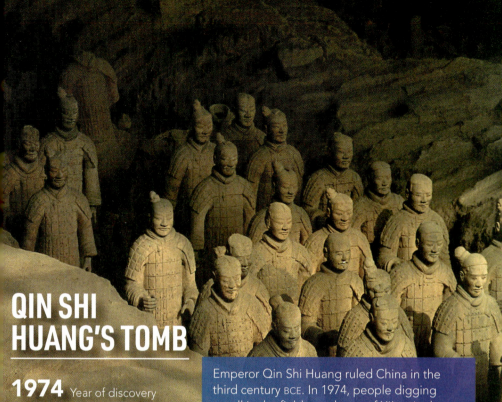

QIN SHI HUANG'S TOMB

1974 Year of discovery

36 Number of years to create

8,000 Total number of figures found

221–210 BCE Duration of Qin Shi Huang's reign

Emperor Qin Shi Huang ruled China in the third century BCE. In 1974, people digging a well in the fields northeast of Xi'an, in the Shaanxi province, accidentally discovered the ancient tomb. Further investigation revealed a burial complex of over 20 square miles. A large pit contained 6,000 life-size terra-cotta warrior figures, each one different from the next and dressed according to rank. A second pit and third contained 2,000 more figures, clay horses, about 40,000 bronze weapons, and other artifacts. Historians think that 700,000 people worked for about thirty-six years to create this incredible mausoleum. The emperor's tomb remains sealed to preserve its contents and to protect workers from possible hazards, such as chemical poisoning from mercury in the surrounding soil.

FIRST EMPEROR OF CHINA

Emperor Qin Shi Huang was the first emperor of a unified China. Before his rule, the territory had been a collection of independent states. He was just forty-nine years old when he died.

SUPER STRUCTURES

WORLD'S LARGEST ANCIENT CASTLE

PRAGUE CASTLE

According to Guinness World Records, Prague Castle, founded in the late-ninth century CE, is the largest ancient castle complex in the world. Covering an area of 750,000 square feet, the castle grounds span enough land for seven football fields, with buildings in various architectural styles that have been added and renovated during past centuries. They include the famous St. Vitus Cathedral. Formerly the home of kings and emperors, the castle is now occupied by the president of the Czech Republic and his family and is also open to tourists.

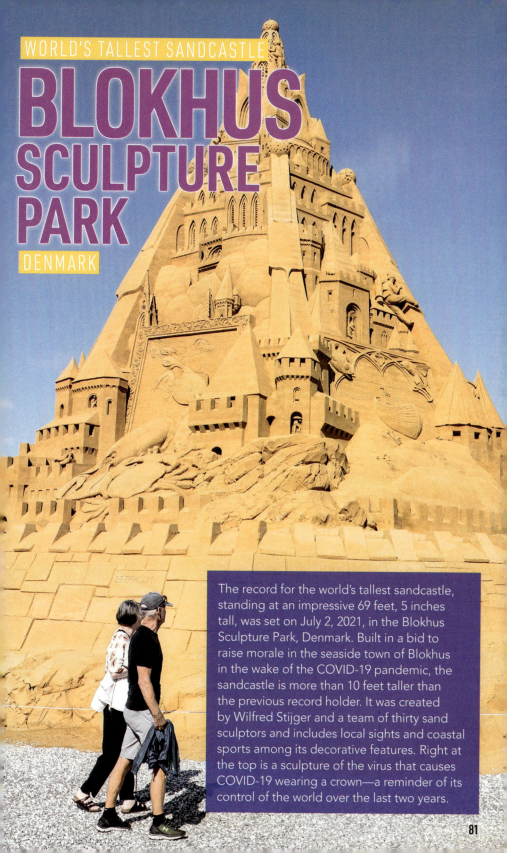

WORLD'S TALLEST SANDCASTLE
BLOKHUS SCULPTURE PARK
DENMARK

The record for the world's tallest sandcastle, standing at an impressive 69 feet, 5 inches tall, was set on July 2, 2021, in the Blokhus Sculpture Park, Denmark. Built in a bid to raise morale in the seaside town of Blokhus in the wake of the COVID-19 pandemic, the sandcastle is more than 10 feet taller than the previous record holder. It was created by Wilfred Stijger and a team of thirty sand sculptors and includes local sights and coastal sports among its decorative features. Right at the top is a sculpture of the virus that causes COVID-19 wearing a crown—a reminder of its control of the world over the last two years.

SUPER STRUCTURES

WORLD'S LONGEST LEGO® SHIP

WORLD DREAM

In 2018, 1,000 cruise passengers and volunteers came together to help build a replica of the *World Dream* cruise ship, a vessel owned by China's Dream Cruises Management Ltd. Boasting more than 2.5 million LEGO® blocks, this spectacle is the longest LEGO® ship ever built. It's a complete scaled-down replica of the *World Dream* cruise ship, with all eighteen of its decks, and measures 27 feet, 8.5 inches in length. Upon completion, it was placed in Hong Kong's Kai Tak Cruise Terminal for all to see.

WORLD'S LARGEST SCULPTURE CUT FROM A SINGLE PIECE OF STONE
SPHINX

The Great Sphinx stands guard near three large pyramids in Giza, Egypt. Historians believe ancient people created the sculpture about 4,500 years ago for the pharaoh Khafre. They carved the sphinx from one mass of limestone in the desert floor, creating a sculpture about 66 feet high and 240 feet long. It has the head of a pharaoh and the body of a lion. The sculpture may represent Ruti, a twin lion god from ancient myths that protected the sun god, Ra, and guarded entrances to the underworld. Sand has covered and preserved the Great Sphinx, but over many years, wind and humidity have worn parts of the soft limestone away, some of which have been restored using blocks of sand and quicklime.

GREAT SPHINX FACTS
Age: **4,500** years (estimated)
Length: **240** feet
Height: **66** feet

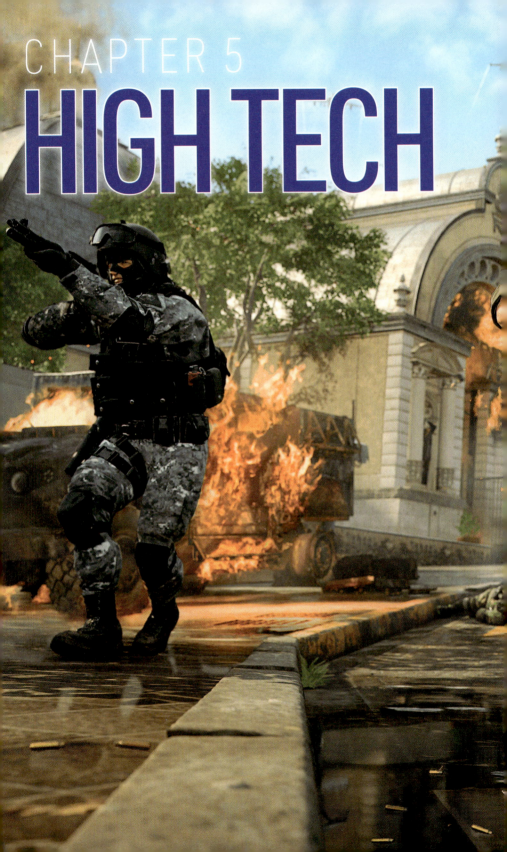

CHAPTER 5
HIGH TECH

HIGH TECH
TRENDING

SPACE DUDE
FIRST YOUTUBER IN SPACE

Coby Cotton, the founder of Dude Perfect, became the first YouTuber to go into space. In 2022, he was one of six passengers in a ten-minute ride on Blue Origin's New Shepard rocket NS-22, reaching an altitude of 350,866 feet. Cotton's amazing experience was funded by cryptocurrency firm MoonDAO, which put out a public vote to see which celebrity it should send. Cotton documented the whole trip in a video on Dude Perfect's YouTube channel, which has been viewed more than 20 million times.

COVID FREE?
PROTESTS IN CHINA LEAD TO DROPPING OF ZERO COVID POLICY

China changed its rules on COVID-19 in December 2022, following mass protests. Before December, China had severe restrictions in place: People were forced to quarantine in government facilities, and lockdowns were strictly enforced. The restrictions were causing people to suffer, with food shortages and a lack of access to medical care. Chinese authorities attempted to shut down protestors by cutting access to non-Chinese social media, but ultimately they had to ease their policies.

RIP, YOUR MAJESTY
DEATH OF ELIZABETH II DOMINATES GLOBAL SOCIAL MEDIA

The passing of the longest-reigning British monarch, Queen Elizabeth II, seemed to be all anyone could talk about in late 2022. Millions of people were informed of her death on September 8 by the royal family's Twitter and Instagram accounts, and the Internet worked fast to spread the news, with the first Wikipedia edit to her page occurring just one minute after the news first broke. Tributes from around the world were posted on social media, along with essays and memes dissecting Elizabeth II's seventy years on the throne.

JUST DID IT
NIKE'S GIANT 3D BILLBOARD

Shinjuku Station in Tokyo, Japan, became home to a giant pair of Nike sneakers in 2022—or did it? In honor of Air Max Day—the 35th anniversary of the shoe's creation—Nike took over the Cross Shinjuku Vision screen, a 1,665-square-foot digital billboard, which displayed Air Maxes being unboxed as a convincing 3D illusion. The campaign ran for a whole week and was hailed as one of the best ads of 2022.

TWITTER TAKEOVER
ELON MUSK BUYS SOCIAL MEDIA SITE

One of the biggest social media stories of 2022 was billionaire Elon Musk's decision to buy Twitter—and the massive problems that followed his takeover. Once the sale went through in November, Musk immediately started making big changes at the company. Twitter apparently lost 52,000 employees, and the instability this caused showed on the app itself, which began introducing and removing features at an unprecedented rate.

HIGH TECH

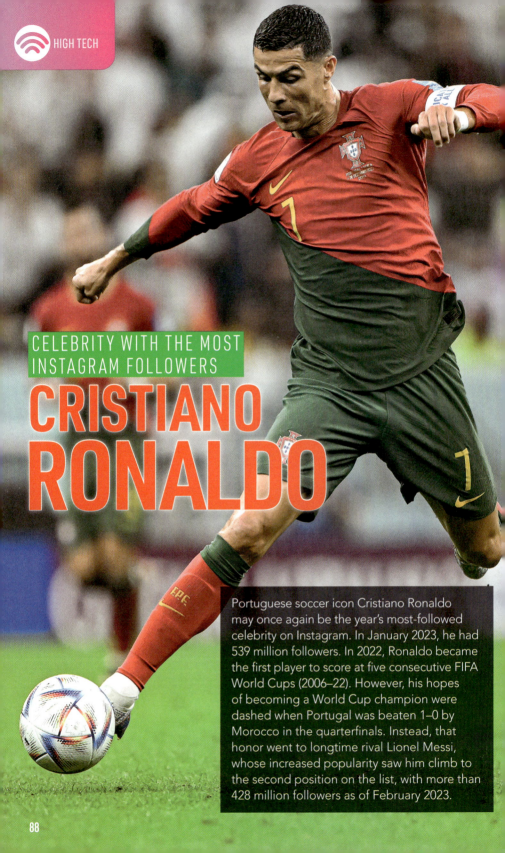

CELEBRITY WITH THE MOST INSTAGRAM FOLLOWERS
CRISTIANO RONALDO

Portuguese soccer icon Cristiano Ronaldo may once again be the year's most-followed celebrity on Instagram. In January 2023, he had 539 million followers. In 2022, Ronaldo became the first player to score at five consecutive FIFA World Cups (2006–22). However, his hopes of becoming a World Cup champion were dashed when Portugal was beaten 1–0 by Morocco in the quarterfinals. Instead, that honor went to longtime rival Lionel Messi, whose increased popularity saw him climb to the second position on the list, with more than 428 million followers as of February 2023.

MOST RETWEETED TWEET EVER
YUSAKU MAEZAWA

Yusaku Maezawa holds the title for most retweeted tweet of all time, with a whopping 4.4 million retweets. Celebrating his company's high Christmas–New Year earnings in 2018–2019, the Japanese billionaire posted a tweet with accompanying images promising to split one hundred million yen ($937,638) among one hundred randomly chosen people. Another giveaway from Yusaku (who tweets as @yousuck2020) also made the list as the second-most retweeted tweet. The prospect of free money definitely helped motivate people to make this one go viral!

HIGH TECH

MOST-DOWNLOADED GAME APP
SUBWAY SURFERS

MOST-DOWNLOADED GAME APPS WORLDWIDE

Subway Surfers: 284 million

Garena Free Fire: 262 million

Stumble Guys: 220 million

Roblox: 188 million

Candy Crush Saga: 168 million

According to app data collator Appmagic, *Subway Surfers* was the most-downloaded game app across the globe in 2022. Launched in May 2012, the endless running game sees you collecting coins while dodging trams, trains, and other moving obstacles, with a security guard hot on your tail. A perennial favorite, the game amassed 284 million downloads. Meanwhile, in February 2023, *Stumble Guys*, claimed the no. 3 spot, ahead of *Roblox* and *Candy Crush Saga*, with more than 220 million downloads since it launched in 2021.

MOST-VIEWED YOUTUBE VIDEO EVER
"BABY SHARK DANCE"

The addictive "Baby Shark Dance" video by South Korean brand Pinkfong (by SmartStudy) has been viewed at least 12 billion times since its upload in June 2016, making it the most-viewed YouTube video ever. The simple song and its accompanying dance moves went viral in 2018, and "Baby Shark Dance" now has its own line of merchandise, as well as an animated series on Nickelodeon. There is even a remix starring Luis Fonsi, which is ironic, given that Fonsi's "Despacito" held the no. 1 spot prior to "Baby Shark Dance."

HIGH TECH

MOST POPULAR NEW EMOJI

FACE HOLDING BACK TEARS

Heart Hands

Melting Face

Face with Peeking Eye

Saluting Face

Pinched Fingers

Face with Hand Over Mouth

Bubbles

Dotted Line Face

Face with Diagonal Mouth

According to online resource Emojipedia, the most popular new emoji in 2022 was Face Holding Back Tears. The announcement was made at the site's World Emoji Awards, which take place annually in celebration of World Emoji Day, July 17. Results are based on Twitter usage with the analysis of more than 463 million tweets. Runners-up in this year's awards were Heart Hands and Melting Face.

MOST-SIGNED CHANGE.ORG PETITION

JUSTICE FOR GEORGE FLOYD

In June 2020, "Justice for George Floyd" became Change.org's most-signed petition ever, with eighteen million signatures. The petition called for the four police officers involved in Floyd's death to be fired and arrested. George Floyd, a Black man, died on May 25 after white officer Derek Chauvin knelt on his neck for almost nine minutes during an arrest, with three fellow officers standing by. Video footage of the event went viral, sparking antiracism protests across the globe. In April 2021, Derek Chauvin was found guilty of three charges for killing George Floyd.

HIGH TECH

ZACH KING

MOST-VIEWED TIKTOK VIDEO

Proving that the world still loves watching magic, three of the five most-viewed videos on the TikTok platform come from American illusionist Zach King. The most popular TikTok video ever, with 2.1 billion views, shows King pulling off a Harry Potter–based trick in which he uses a longboard and mirrored surface to create the illusion of flying on a broomstick down a California street. The only TikToks in the top five that are not by King come from makeup YouTuber James Charles, with his "Sisters Christmas Party" (2019), which has nearly 2 billion views, and Bella Poarch's "M To The B" video (2020) with more than 730 million views.

FIRST ACCOUNT TO REACH 100M ON TIKTOK

CHARLI D'AMELIO

Charli D'Amelio became the first TikTok user to hit one hundred million followers on the app in November 2020, when she was only sixteen years old. The social media personality, who joined the app in 2019, quickly became known for her lip-syncing and dancing challenge videos. Her one hundred million milestone came at a controversial time, with D'Amelio losing around one million followers for her behavior in a "Dinner with the D'Amelios" YouTube segment. Despite this, D'Amelio's online presence has earned her an estimated net worth of $8 million, including income from movie roles and brand partnerships.

HIGH TECH

DOG WITH THE MOST INSTAGRAM FOLLOWERS
JIFFPOM

On May 3, 2017, and with 4.8 million followers, Jiffpom broke the Guinness World Record for being the most popular dog on Instagram. Six years later, as of March 2023, the dog's follower count was at the 9.7-million mark. Jiffpom's owner posts snapshots of the fluffy little dog dressed in cute outfits, and Jiffpom even has a website. The Pomeranian from the United States has other records to boast of, too. At one time, he held the record for fastest dog to cover a distance of 16.4 feet on his front legs (7.76 seconds). Another time, he was the record holder for covering 32.8 feet on his hind legs (6.56 seconds).

CAT WITH THE MOST INSTAGRAM FOLLOWERS

NALA CAT

In January 2020, and with a total of 4.3 million followers, Nala Cat broke the Guinness World Record for cat with the most followers on Instagram. As of February 2023, the feline remains just as popular with 4.4 million. Adopted from a shelter at just five months old, the Siamese-Tabby charms online viewers around the world with her bright blue eyes and supercute headgear.

HIGH TECH

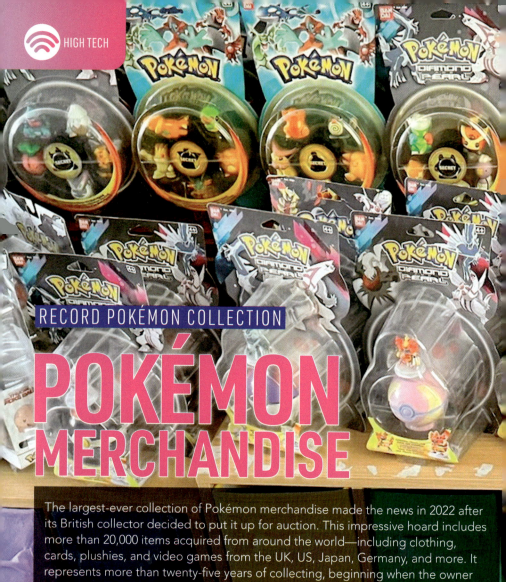

RECORD POKÉMON COLLECTION

POKÉMON MERCHANDISE

The largest-ever collection of Pokémon merchandise made the news in 2022 after its British collector decided to put it up for auction. This impressive hoard includes more than 20,000 items acquired from around the world—including clothing, cards, plushies, and video games from the UK, US, Japan, Germany, and more. It represents more than twenty-five years of collecting, beginning when the owner was just nine years old. Some of the rarer (and stranger!) things she found include cans of Pokémon-shaped spaghetti and even Pokémon-printed toilet paper! All of these treasures were due to be auctioned in Derbyshire, UK, in October 2022, at a reserve price of £300,000. Despite the high demand for Pokémon items, this was too high a price to pay for even the most avid collector, and the lot failed to sell.

HIGH TECH

BEST-SELLING
VIDEO GAME EVER

TETRIS

Tetris, developed by Russian computer scientist Alexey Pajitnov in 1984, has sold over 500 million copies worldwide—more than any other game. It has been available on almost every video game console since its creation and has seen a resurgence in sales as an app for cell phones and tablets. The iconic puzzle game was the first video game to be exported from the Soviet Union to the United States, the first to be played in outer space, and is often listed as one of the best video games of all time. In 2019, Nintendo released *Tetris 99* for Nintendo Switch—a multiplayer version of the game that sees ninety-nine players compete against one another online.

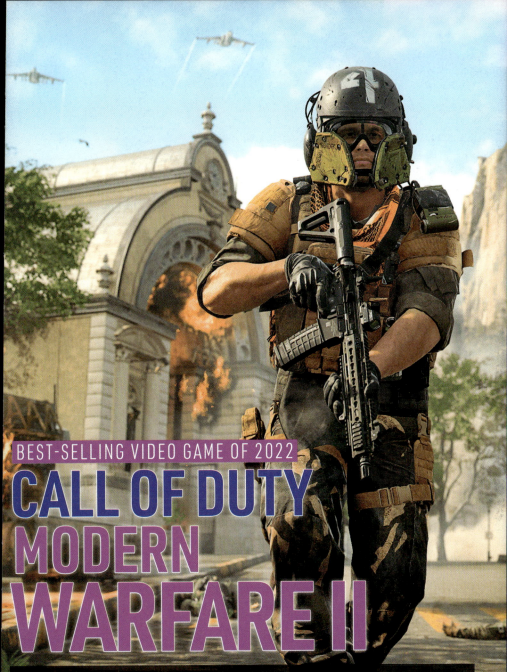

BEST-SELLING VIDEO GAME OF 2022
CALL OF DUTY MODERN WARFARE II

Issued by Activision Blizzard, *Call of Duty* video games have led sales in the United States for the last three years. In 2022, it was the turn of *Call of Duty: Modern Warfare II*—a rebooted version of a game initially launched in 2009—to top the list, despite only having been available since October. Its predecessor, *Call of Duty: Black Ops Cold War* didn't even make the top five, which instead featured *Elden Ring*, *Madden NFL 23*, *God of War*, and *LEGO Star Wars*. Since its inception in 2003, *Call of Duty* has sold more than 400 million units worldwide and is second only to *Tetris* as the best-selling video game ever.

HIGH TECH

BEST-SELLING CONSOLE OF ALL TIME PS2

PlayStation's legendary console, the PS2, is still the best-selling console of all time, with parent company Sony confirming the sale of more than 158 million units. Launched in 2000, the PS2 was particularly successful because it could play PS2 games, PS1 games, and even DVDs. More modern consoles have struggled to match the PS2's success; in fact, the majority of the top 10 best-selling consoles are more than a decade old. In second place, with around 155 million units sold, is the Nintendo DS, released in 2004, and in third place is 1989's classic Game Boy, which sold 118.69 million units before it was discontinued fourteen years later.

BEST-SELLING VIDEO GAME FRANCHISE OF ALL TIME
MARIO

Nintendo's *Mario* franchise has sold 681 million units since the first game was released in 1981. Since then, Mario, his brother Luigi, and other characters like Princess Peach and Yoshi have become household names, starring in a number of games. In the early games, like *Super Mario World*, players jump over obstacles, collect tokens, and capture flags as Mario journeys through the Mushroom Kingdom to save the princess. The franchise has since diversified to include other popular games, such as *Mario Kart*, a racing game showcasing the inhabitants and landscapes of the Mushroom Kingdom.

BEST-SELLING VIDEO GAME FRANCHISES
Units sold in millions

- *Mario* (Nintendo)
- *Tetris* (The Tetris Company)
- *Call of Duty* (Activision)
- *Pokémon* (Game Freak)
- *Grand Theft Auto* (Rockstar North)

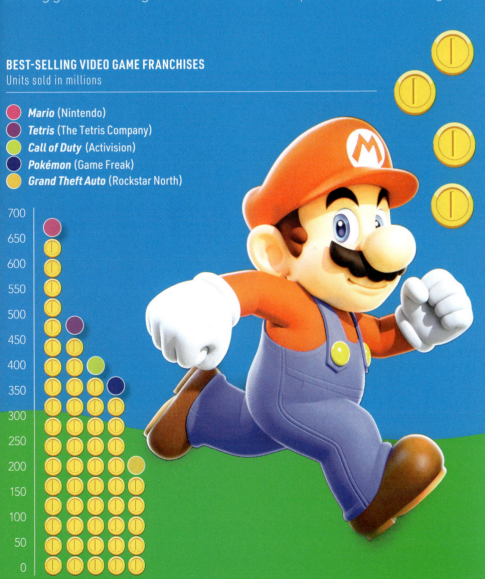

HIGH TECH

MINEFAIRE STATS:

12,140 Number of people attending Minefaire

150,000 Total area, in square feet, of Minecraft-centered attractions

3 Number of Guinness World Records broken at the fair

BIGGEST CONVENTION FOR A SINGLE VIDEO GAME
MINEFAIRE 2016

According to Guinness World Records, Minefaire 2016, a huge gathering of *Minecraft* fans, was the biggest convention ever for a single video game. Held October 15–16 at the Greater Philadelphia Expo Center in Oaks, Pennsylvania, the event attracted 12,140 people. Game developer Markus Persson created *Minecraft* in 2009 and sold it to Microsoft in 2014 for $2.5 billion. Gamers can play alone or with other players online. The game involves breaking and placing blocks to build whatever gamers can imagine—from simple constructions to huge virtual worlds. Attendance was not the only element of Minefaire to gain world-record status. On October 15, the largest-ever *Minecraft* architecture lesson attracted 342 attendees, and American gamer Lestat Wade broke the record for building the tallest staircase in *Minecraft* in one minute.

HIGH TECH

TOP-EARNING YOUTUBER
MRBEAST

Jimmy Donaldson, better known as MrBeast, is famed for his outlandish and generous YouTube giveaways—$10,000 to sit in a bathtub of snakes, anyone?—so it should surprise nobody that he's also raking in the cash. In 2021, his $54 million in earnings made him the highest-grossing YouTuber of all time. He also made a bold foray into the food industry, creating the "MrBeast Burger" virtual restaurant brand, which partners with existing restaurants around the United States to make and deliver his menu.

WORLD'S SMALLEST SURGICAL ROBOT
VERSIUS

British robot specialist Cambridge Medical Robotics developed the world's smallest surgical robot in 2017. Operated by a surgeon using a console guide with a 3D screen, the robot is able to carry out keyhole surgery. The scientists modeled the robot, called Versius, on the human arm, giving it similar wrist joints to allow maximum flexibility. Keyhole surgery involves making very small cuts on the surface of a person's body, through which a surgeon can then operate. The recovery time of the patient is usually quicker when operated on in this way.

HIGH TECH

BIGGEST WALKING ROBOT

FANNY

Fanny is a massive 26-foot-high, 51-foot-long, fire-breathing dragon. She is also the world's biggest walking robot. In 2012, a German company designed and built Fanny using both hydraulic and electronic parts. She is radio remote-controlled with nine controllers, while 238 sensors allow the robot to assess her environment.

She does this while walking on her four legs or stretching wings that span 39 feet. Powered by a 140-horsepower diesel engine, Fanny weighs a hefty 24,250 pounds—as much as two elephants—and breathes real fire using 24 pounds of liquid gas.

FANNY STATS:

09/27/2012 Date of Fanny's launch

26´10˝ Fanny's height in feet and inches

51´6˝ Fanny's length in feet and inches

12´ Fanny's body width in feet

39´ Fanny's wingspan in feet

CHAPTER 6
AMAZING ANIMALS

AMAZING ANIMALS
TRENDING

SAY HELLO
NEW SPECIES IDENTIFIED IN 2022

According to the California Academy of Sciences, 146 new species (animal and plant) were added to its records in 2022—and nearly a third of them were lizards. Two of the new species were discovered by high schoolers Harper Forbes and Prakrit Jain, who first spotted the scorpion species *Paruroctonus soda* and *Paruroctonus conclusus* on the iNaturalist social network before finding them in real life.

TAKEOUT
CAMEL VISITS DRIVE-THRU

In-N-Out Burger's famous "animal fries" got a whole new meaning in October when Brandon Nobles filmed his camel getting french fries from a drive-thru in Las Vegas. The camel, Fergie, is a twelve-year-old rescue from a camel dairy farm in Colorado who now lives in Nevada with her foster family and several horses. #FergieTheCamel's adventures are documented on Instagram at @jeffrys_farm, with pictures of her enjoying being "socialized" at local food joints such as Chipotle and Einstein Bros. Bagels.

A GREAT ESCAPE?
ZOO ANIMALS CAUGHT IN CONFLICT

The Russian invasion of Ukraine in February 2022 didn't just force humans out of their homes. Many animals in the country's zoos were relocated for their own safety, including eighty animals from the Kyiv Zoo that survived a difficult journey into Poland. A majority of the animals in the nation's three biggest zoos, however, stayed put, and their keepers moved them underground or sedated them to help them cope with the stress of nearby bombs and fighting sounds.

MOOSE MALFUNCTION
VIRAL VIDEO SHOWS ANTLER CASTING

A TikTok video of a moose gained 18 million views in a week after an Alaskan woman posted footage from her Ring doorbell. These doorbell cameras react to motion, which triggers them to start recording. In this case, the motion was a moose walking by, scratching its hind legs, and startling itself into a run when its antlers came off with a sudden popping sound. Moose antlers are shed (or "cast") every winter before regrowing in spring.

BEAR-Y DELICIOUS
HUNGRY BEAR STEALS BAGELS FROM PORCH

In another piece of viral doorbell-camera footage, a woman in Hendersonville, North Carolina, caught a very furry thief stealing a recently delivered bagel care package from her front porch in December 2022. The bear took the entire box without even breaking into it to check the contents! The 25-second clip of the theft was posted on Facebook by a local news channel and viewed 19,000 times in the month that followed.

AMAZING ANIMALS

WORLD'S SLEEPIEST ANIMAL
KOALA

Australia's koala sleeps for up to twenty hours a day and still manages to look sleepy when awake. This is due to the koala's unbelievably monotonous diet. It feeds, mostly at night, on the aromatic leaves of eucalyptus trees. The leaves have little nutritional or caloric value, so the marsupial saves energy by snoozing. It jams its rear end into a fork in the branches of its favorite tree so that it cannot fall out while asleep.

FLYING SQUIRREL

WORLD'S BEST GLIDER

Flying squirrels are champion animal gliders. The Japanese giant flying squirrel has been scientifically recorded making flights over distances of up to 164 feet from tree to tree. These creatures have been estimated to make 656-foot flights when flying downhill. The squirrel remains aloft using a special flap of skin on either side of its body, which stretches between its wrist and ankle. Its fluffy tail acts as a stabilizer to keep it steady, and the squirrel changes direction by twisting its wrists and moving its limbs.

WORLD'S GLIDERS
Distance in feet

- Flying squirrel
- Flying fish
- Colugo, or flying lemur
- Draco, or flying lizard
- Flying squid

164   197   230   655   656

115

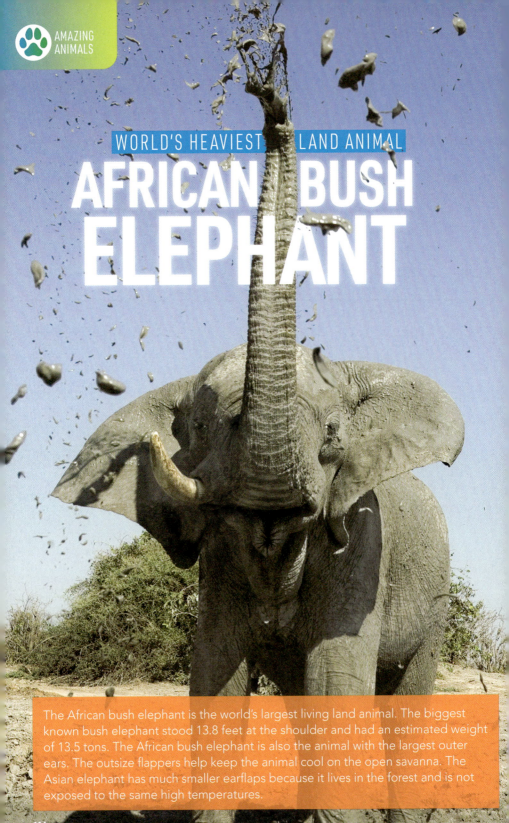

AMAZING ANIMALS

WORLD'S HEAVIEST LAND ANIMAL
AFRICAN BUSH ELEPHANT

The African bush elephant is the world's largest living land animal. The biggest known bush elephant stood 13.8 feet at the shoulder and had an estimated weight of 13.5 tons. The African bush elephant is also the animal with the largest outer ears. The outsize flappers help keep the animal cool on the open savanna. The Asian elephant has much smaller earflaps because it lives in the forest and is not exposed to the same high temperatures.

WORLD'S TINIEST BAT

KITTI'S HOG-NOSED BAT

This little critter, the Kitti's hog-nosed bat, measures just 1.3 inches long, with a wingspan of 6.7 inches, and weighs 0.07–0.10 ounces. It's tied for first place as the world's smallest mammal with Savi's Etruscan shrew, which is longer at 2.1 inches but lighter at 0.04–0.06 ounces. The bat lives in west-central Thailand and southeast Myanmar, and the shrew is found in areas from the Mediterranean to Southeast Asia.

AMAZING ANIMALS

WORLD'S LARGEST PRIMATE

GORILLA

The largest living primates on Earth are the eastern gorillas, and the biggest subspecies among them is the very rare mountain gorilla. The tallest known was an adult male silverback, named for the color of the fur on his back. He stood at 6.4 feet tall, but he was an exception—silverbacks generally grow no bigger than 5.9 feet tall. Gorillas have long arms. The record holder had an arm span measuring 8.9 feet, while adult male humans have an average arm span of just 5.9 feet.

WORLD'S MOST COLORFUL MONKEY

MANDRILL

The male mandrill's face is as flamboyant as his rear end. The vivid colors of both are brightest at breeding time. The colors announce to his rivals that he is an alpha male and he has the right to breed with the females. His exceptionally long and fang-like canine teeth reinforce his dominance. The mandrill is the world's largest monkey, as well as the most colorful.

AMAZING ANIMALS

WORLD'S FASTEST LAND ANIMAL
CHEETAH

The fastest reliably recorded running speed of any animal was that of a zoo-bred cheetah that reached an incredible 61 miles per hour on a flat surface. The record was achieved in 2012 from a standing start by a captive cheetah at the Cincinnati Zoo. More recently, wild cheetahs have been timed while actually hunting their prey in the bush in Botswana. Using GPS technology and special tracking collars, the scientists found that these cheetahs had a top speed of 58 miles per hour over rough terrain.

FASTEST LAND ANIMALS
Top speed

Animal	Speed
Cheetah	61 mph
Ostrich	60 mph
Pronghorn	55 mph
Springbok	55 mph
Lion	30 mph

TIGER
WORLD'S LARGEST BIG CAT

There are only five big cats that roam Earth: tiger, lion, jaguar, leopard, and snow leopard. The biggest and heaviest is the Siberian, or Amur, tiger, which lives in the taiga (boreal forest) of eastern Siberia, where it hunts deer and wild boar. The largest reliably measured tigers have been about 11.8 feet long and weighed 705 pounds, but there have been claims for larger individuals, such as the male shot in the Sikhote-Alin Mountains in 1950. That tiger weighed 847 pounds.

GIRAFFE STATS

6 HEIGHT OF A CALF AT BIRTH IN FEET

25 AVERAGE LIFE SPAN IN YEARS

100 ADULT'S DAILY FOOD CONSUMPTION IN POUNDS OF LEAVES AND TWIGS

WORLD'S TALLEST LIVING ANIMAL
GIRAFFE

Giraffes living on the savannas of eastern and southern Africa are the world's tallest animals. The tallest known bull giraffe measured 19 feet from the ground to the top of his horns. He could have looked over the top of a London double-decker bus or peered into the upstairs window of a two-story house. Despite having considerably longer necks than we do, giraffes have the same number of neck vertebrae. They also have long legs, with which they can either speedily escape from predators or kick them to keep them away.

REACHING GREAT HEIGHTS

A giraffe's tongue can grow up to 21 inches in length. This helps the animal reach leaves on the topmost branches of a tree when it is looking for food.

AMAZING ANIMALS

WORLD'S NOISIEST LAND ANIMAL
HOWLER MONKEY

The howler monkeys of Latin America are deafening. Males have an especially large hyoid bone. This horseshoe-shaped bone in the neck creates a chamber that makes the monkey's deep guttural growls sound louder for longer. It is said that their calls can be heard up to 3 miles away. Both males and females call, and they holler mainly in the morning. It is thought that these calls are often one troop of monkeys telling neighboring troops where they are.

THE ONLY SHARK KNOWN TO WALK ON LAND
EPAULETTE SHARK

On Australia's Great Barrier Reef, and off the coasts of Indonesia and Papua New Guinea, lives a member of the carpet shark family that can walk! Called the epaulette shark, it is recognizable by a black spot, edged in white, on either side of its body. No more than 3 feet long, it lives in the intertidal zone, and when the tide goes out, it is often left stranded in a rock pool. As the temperature of the water rises in the heat, oxygen levels sink. But when oxygen levels get too low for the shark to survive, it uses its paddle-shaped pectoral fins to pull itself over the rocks from one pool to the next, until it finds one with more oxygen in the water.

AMAZING ANIMALS

WORLD'S LONGEST TOOTH

NARWHAL

The narwhal's "sword" is an enormously elongated spiral tooth, or tusk. In male narwhals it can grow to more than 8.2 feet long. Only about 15 percent of females grow a tusk, which typically is smaller than a male tusk, with a less noticeable spiral. It has been suggested that the tusk serves as an adornment to attract the opposite sex—the larger a male narwhal's tusk, the more attractive he is to females. It is also thought to be a sensory organ that detects changes in the seawater, such as saltiness, which could help the narwhal find food. Observers have also noted that the narwhal uses its tusk to stun prey.

THE WORLD'S LARGEST LIVING ANIMAL
BLUE WHALE

Blue whales are truly colossal. The largest one accurately measured was 110 feet long, and the heaviest weighed 209 tons. They feed on tiny krill, which they filter from the sea. On land, the largest known animal was a titanosaur—a huge dinosaur that lived 101 million years ago in what is now Argentina. A skeleton found in 2014 suggests the creature was 121 feet long and weighed 77 tons. It belongs to a young titanosaur, so an adult may have been bigger than a blue whale.

AMAZING ANIMALS

WORLD'S BIGGEST FISH

WHALE SHARK

Recognizable from its spotted skin and enormous size, the whale shark is the world's largest living fish. It grows to a maximum length of about 66 feet. Like the blue whale, this fish feeds on some of the smallest creatures: krill, marine larvae, small fish, and fish eggs. The whale shark is also a great traveler. One female was tracked swimming 4,800 miles from Mexico—where hundreds of whale sharks gather each summer to feed—to the middle of the South Atlantic Ocean, where it is thought she may have given birth.

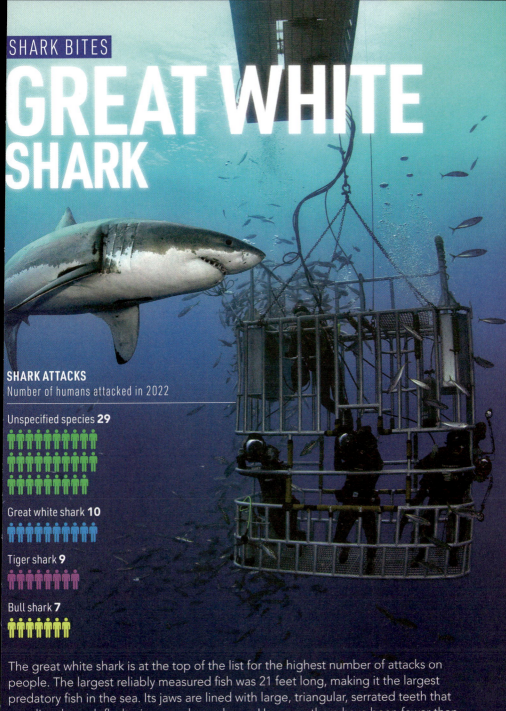

SHARK BITES
GREAT WHITE SHARK

SHARK ATTACKS
Number of humans attacked in 2022

Unspecified species **29**

Great white shark **10**

Tiger shark **9**

Bull shark **7**

The great white shark is at the top of the list for the highest number of attacks on people. The largest reliably measured fish was 21 feet long, making it the largest predatory fish in the sea. Its jaws are lined with large, triangular, serrated teeth that can slice through flesh, sinew, and even bone. However, there have been fewer than 550 reported unprovoked shark attacks in the last ten years, with just 69 of those occurring in 2022. Only eight of those proved fatal. Humans are not this creature's top food of choice. People don't have enough fat on their bodies. Mature white sharks prefer blubber-rich seals, dolphins, and whales. It is likely that many of the attacks on people are probably cases of mistaken identity.

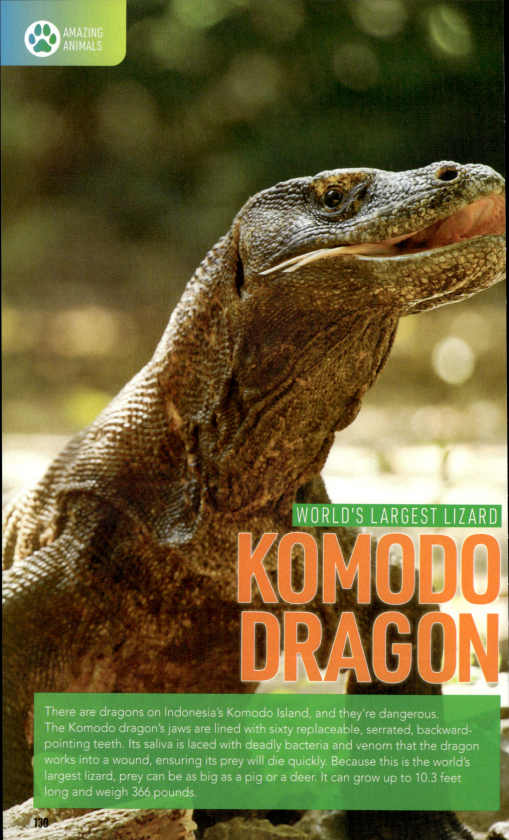

AMAZING ANIMALS

WORLD'S LARGEST LIZARD

KOMODO DRAGON

There are dragons on Indonesia's Komodo Island, and they're dangerous. The Komodo dragon's jaws are lined with sixty replaceable, serrated, backward-pointing teeth. Its saliva is laced with deadly bacteria and venom that the dragon works into a wound, ensuring its prey will die quickly. Because this is the world's largest lizard, prey can be as big as a pig or a deer. It can grow up to 10.3 feet long and weigh 366 pounds.

POISON DART FROG

WORLD'S DEADLIEST FROG

A poison dart frog's skin exudes toxins. There are several species, and the more vivid a frog's color, the more deadly its poison. The skin color warns potential predators that the frogs are not good to eat, although one snake is immune to the chemicals and happily feeds on these creatures. It is thought that the frogs do not manufacture their own poisons, but obtain the chemicals from their diet of ants, millipedes, and mites. The most deadly species to people is also the largest: Colombia's golden poison dart frog. At just 1 inch long, a single frog has enough poison to kill ten to twenty people.

AMAZING ANIMALS

WORLD'S LARGEST REPTILE
SALTWATER CROCODILE

The saltwater crocodile, or "saltie," is the world's largest living reptile. Males can grow to over 20 feet long, but a few old-timers become real monsters. A well-known crocodile in the Segama River, Borneo, left an impression on a sandbank that measured 33 feet. The saltie can be found in areas from eastern India to northeastern Australia, where it lives in mangroves, estuaries, and rivers. It is sometimes found out at sea. The saltie is an ambush predator, grabbing any animal that enters its domain—including people. Saltwater crocodiles account for twenty to thirty attacks on people per year, up to half of which are fatal.

WORLD'S SMALLEST REPTILE
NANO-CHAMELEON

In a mountain forest in northern Madagascar lives the smallest known reptile in the world: the nano-chameleon *Brookesia nana*. From his snout to the tip of his tail, the male of the species is just 0.85 inches long—that's roughly the length of a sunflower seed. The female is a little longer: 1.14 inches. They live among the leaf litter on the forest floor, where they hunt for mites and springtails. They are well camouflaged with a light brown and gray body, and they hide from predators among blades of grass. Unlike most chameleons, they do not change color, but they do have the chameleon's exceptionally long, extendable tongue to capture prey.

AMAZING ANIMALS

WORLD'S SMELLIEST BIRD

HOATZIN

The hoatzin eats leaves, flowers, and fruit. It ferments the food in its crop (a pouch in its esophagus). This habit leaves the bird with a foul odor, which has led people to nickname the hoatzin the "stinkbird." About the size of a pheasant, this bird lives in the Amazon and Orinoco river basins of South America. A hoatzin chick has sharp claws on its wings, like a pterodactyl. If threatened by a snake, the chick jumps from the nest into the water, using its wing claws to help it climb back up.

BIRD WITH THE LONGEST TAIL
RIBBON-TAILED ASTRAPIA

The ribbon-tailed astrapia has the longest feathers in relation to body size of any wild bird. The male, which has a beautiful, iridescent blue-green head, sports a pair of white ribbon-shaped tail feathers that are more than 3.3 feet long—three times the length of its 13-inch-long body. It is one of Papua New Guinea's birds of paradise and lives in the mountain forests of central New Guinea, where males sometimes have to untangle their tails from the foliage before they can fly.

AMAZING ANIMALS

BIRD THAT BUILDS THE LARGEST NEST

BALD EAGLE

With a wingspan of more than 6.6 feet, bald eagles need space to land and take off—so their nests can be gargantuan. Over the years, a nest built by a pair of bald eagles in St. Petersburg, Florida, has taken on epic proportions. Measuring 9.5 feet across and 20 feet deep, it is made of sticks, grass, and moss. At one stage, it was thought to have weighed at least 2 tons, making it the largest nest ever constructed by a pair of birds. Although one pair nests at a time, these huge structures are often the work of several pairs of birds, each building on top of the work of their predecessors.

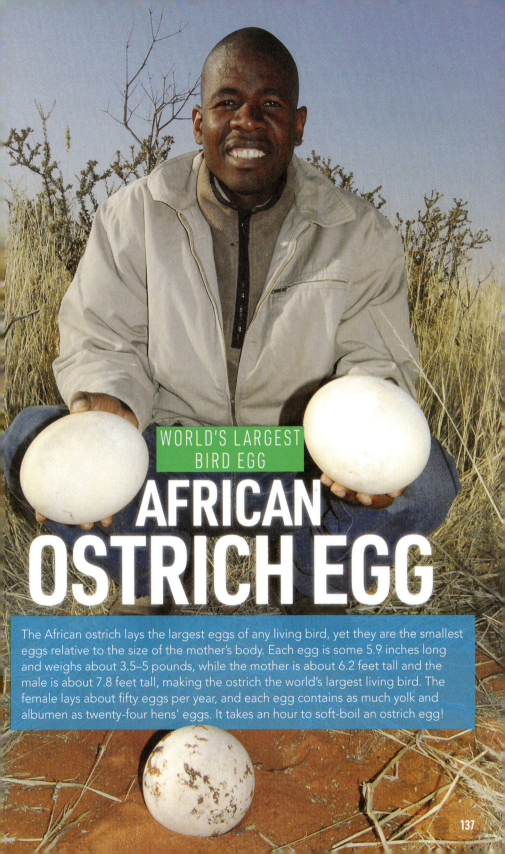

WORLD'S LARGEST BIRD EGG
AFRICAN OSTRICH EGG

The African ostrich lays the largest eggs of any living bird, yet they are the smallest eggs relative to the size of the mother's body. Each egg is some 5.9 inches long and weighs about 3.5–5 pounds, while the mother is about 6.2 feet tall and the male is about 7.8 feet tall, making the ostrich the world's largest living bird. The female lays about fifty eggs per year, and each egg contains as much yolk and albumen as twenty-four hens' eggs. It takes an hour to soft-boil an ostrich egg!

EMPEROR PENGUIN STATS

80 AVERAGE WEIGHT OF AN ADULT IN POUNDS

1,751 DEPTH AN ADULT CAN SWIM TO IN FEET

22 LENGTH OF TIME UNDERWATER IN MINUTES

FIVE OF THE WORLD'S PENGUINS
Height in inches

Emperor	48
King	39
Gentoo	35
Macaroni	28
Galápagos	19

WORLD'S BIGGEST PENGUIN
EMPEROR PENGUIN

At 4 feet tall, the emperor penguin is the world's biggest living penguin. It has a most curious lifestyle, breeding during the long, dark Antarctic winter. The female lays a single egg and carefully passes it to the male. She then heads out to sea to feed, while he remains with the egg balanced on his feet and tucked under a fold of blubber-rich skin. There he stands with all the other penguin dads, huddled together to keep warm in the blizzards and 100-mile-per-hour winds that scour the icy continent. Come spring, the egg hatches, the female returns, and Mom and Dad swap duties, taking turns feeding and caring for their fluffy chick.

AMAZING ANIMALS

WORLD'S HEAVIEST SPIDER
GOLIATH BIRD-EATING TARANTULA

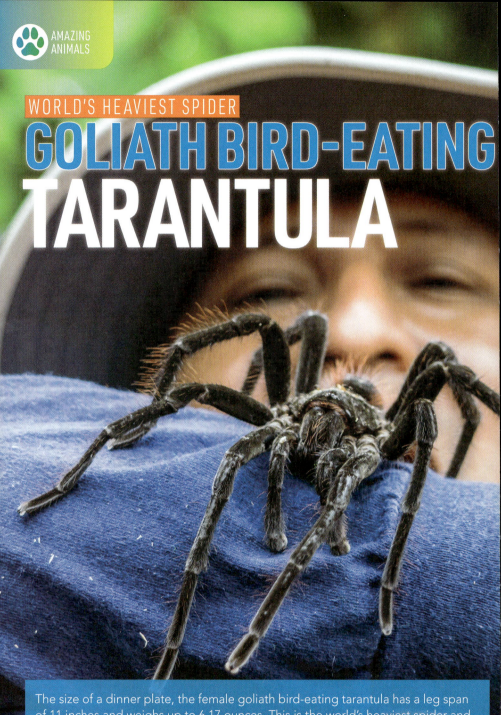

The size of a dinner plate, the female goliath bird-eating tarantula has a leg span of 11 inches and weighs up to 6.17 ounces. This is the world's heaviest spider and a real nightmare for an arachnophobe (someone with a fear of spiders). Its fangs can pierce a person's skin, but its venom is no worse than a bee sting. The hairs on its body are more of a hazard. When threatened, it rubs its abdomen with its hind legs and releases tiny hairs that cause severe irritation to the skin. Despite its name, this spider does not actually eat birds very often.

WORLD'S BIGGEST HORNET

ASIAN GIANT HORNET

At 2 inches long, with a ¼-inch stinger and fearsome jaws, the Asian giant hornet is more than twice the size of other hornet species. It is also very aggressive, earning the nickname "murder hornet." While native to Asia, this hornet is also known in the Pacific Northwest, where several nests have been discovered since 2019. The hornet's prime target is the honeybee. A swarm of giant hornets can kill bees at a rate of one every 14 seconds and wipe out an entire hive in only a couple of hours. This is a problem for farmers, whose crops need honeybees to pollinate them. In the Pacific Northwest, for example, honeybees are crucial to the successful harvest of cherries, apples, and blueberries. Thankfully, the hornet nests are a rare sight in the United States and farmers are developing ways to protect their bees.

AMAZING ANIMALS

WORLD'S FASTEST KNOWN ANIMAL MOVEMENT IN NATURE
DRACULA ANT

The Dracula ant, *Mystrium camillae*, of tropical areas of Africa, Southeast Asia, and Australasia, makes the fastest movement of any known animal on Earth. In the time it takes you to blink, it can open and close its jaws *five thousand* times. It does this by pressing its jaws together, storing energy like a spring, and then sliding them past each other at up to 200 miles per hour. Such fast jaws allow the ant to stun or kill its prey, such as fast-moving centipedes, which have their own formidable jaws!

WORLD'S FASTEST FLYING INSECT
DESERT LOCUST

Flying insects are difficult to clock, and many impressive speeds have been claimed over the years. The fastest airspeed reliably timed was by fifteen desert locusts that managed an average of 21 miles per hour. Airspeed is the actual speed at which the insect flies. It is different from ground speed, which is often enhanced by favorable winds. A black cutworm moth whizzed along at 70 miles per hour while riding the winds ahead of a cold front. The most shocking measurement, however, is that of a horsefly with an estimated airspeed of 90 miles per hour while chasing an air-gun pellet! Understandably, this is one speed that has not been verified!

AMAZING ANIMALS

WORLD'S DEADLIEST ANIMAL
MOSQUITO

Female mosquitoes live on the blood of birds and mammals—humans included. However, the problem is not what they take, but what they leave behind. In some mosquitoes' saliva are organisms that cause the world's most deadly illnesses, including malaria, yellow fever, dengue fever, West Nile virus, and encephalitis. It is estimated that mosquitoes transmit diseases to 700 million people every year, of which 725,000 die. In 2021, the World Health Organization (WHO) announced the release of a vaccine that can help prevent a mosquito-borne disease called malaria, and that has the potential to save tens of thousands of lives.

WORLD'S LONGEST INSECT MIGRATION

GLOBE SKIMMER

Each year, millions of dragonflies fly thousands of miles across the Indian Ocean from South India to East Africa. Most of them are globe skimmers, a species known to fly long distances and at altitudes up to 3,280 feet. They can travel 2,175 miles in 24 hours. Coral cays on the way have little open fresh water, so the insects stay there for a few days before moving on to East Africa. Here, they follow the rains, at each stop taking advantage of temporary rainwater pools to lay their eggs to hatch where their young can rapidly develop. Four generations are involved in a round trip of about 11,000 miles—farther than the distance from New York City to Sydney.

AMAZING PETS
TRENDING

ALONE NO MORE
FISHTOPHER THE CAT STEALS THE INTERNET'S HEARTS

The description of a cat available for adoption went viral on Twitter in 2022, bringing crowds of cat lovers to a New Jersey animal shelter. Five-year-old Fishtopher was described as so depressed he could only eat with company, and people immediately fell in love with his sad eyes and big cheeks. Potential adopters waited in line at the shelter to meet him, and he was soon adopted by a couple who have been documenting his new life on both Instagram and Twitter.

EMMANUEL: NO!
TIKTOK BIRD SURVIVES FLU OUTBREAK

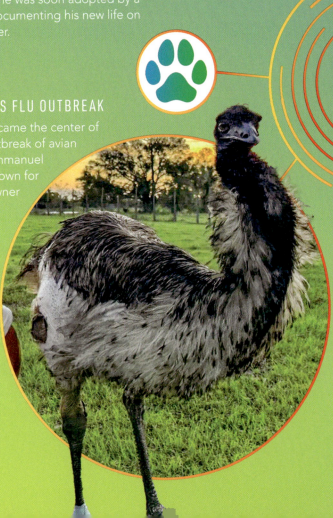

A famous TikTok emu became the center of a controversy after an outbreak of avian flu at his owner's farm. Emmanuel Todd Lopez is an emu known for his cheeky behavior in owner Taylor Blake's videos, but Blake's posts took a sad turn when she revealed a number of her birds had been culled to stop the flu from spreading. However, despite Emmanuel having had the virus, too, local authorities had allowed him to live, suggesting that the bird's TikTok fame led Blake to break the rules.

146

LICENSE TO CUTE
AN UNUSUAL REQUEST FOR ANIMAL CONTROL

A six-year-old girl might be the first person ever issued a license to own a unicorn in her backyard. Madeline, who lives in Los Angeles County, California, wrote a letter to the LA County Department of Animal Care and Control asking for permission to keep one of the magical creatures—if she ever found one. The director of animal control was so impressed by her initiative that she immediately sent Madeline a pink certificate of approval!

RESCUED PUPS
DOGS SURVIVE PLANE CRASH

Tragedy nearly struck in 2022 when a plane carrying rescue dogs from Louisiana to Wisconsin crashed near Milwaukee. A local animal shelter rescued all fifty-three dogs from the crash—and was immediately inundated with phone calls from people wanting to adopt the pups and send the shelter money for their care. The Humane Animal Welfare Society of Waukesha County (HAWS) put up a fundraising drive on Facebook, and was shocked to raise more than $2,600 on the very first day.

ADOPT, DON'T SHOP
NEW YORK OUTLAWS SELLING PETS IN STORES

A new law was passed in New York State preventing the sale of dogs, cats, and rabbits in pet stores. This law, which will go into effect in 2024, is intended to bring a halt to inhumane setups like puppy mills, which breed many dogs in poor conditions to sell to shops for profit. Instead, pet stores are being encouraged to work with animal shelters to give homes to pets that need a second chance.

AMAZING ANIMALS

WORLD'S FLUFFIEST RABBIT
ANGORA RABBIT

In most people's opinion, the Angora rabbit is the world's fluffiest bunny. The breed originated in Turkey and is thought to be one of the world's oldest rabbit breeds as well. It became popular with the French court in the mid-eighteenth century. Today, it is bred for its long, soft wool, which is shorn every three to four months. One of the fluffiest bunnies ever was buff-colored Franchesca, owned by English Angora rabbit expert Dr. Betty Chu. In 2014, Franchesca's fur was measured at 14.37 inches, a world record that has yet to be beaten.

LITTLEST HORSE BREED
FALABELLA

Originally bred in Argentina, the Falabella miniature horse is the world's smallest recognized breed of horse. While newborn foals can be 12–22 inches tall at the withers (the ridge between the shoulder blades), adults mature at 25–34 inches. They are proportionally similar to other horses, and not ponies, except they are tiny; and they have seventeen vertebrae in their backbone rather than the usual eighteen. Bay (brown body with a black mane and tail) and black are the most common colors, but there are pintos, palominos, and spotted individuals resembling Appaloosas.

AMAZING ANIMALS

WORLD'S HAIRIEST DOG
KOMONDOR

The world's hairiest dog breed is the Komondor, or Hungarian sheepdog. It is a powerful dog that was bred originally to guard sheep. Its long, white, dreadlock-like "cords" enable it not only to blend in with the flock but also to protect itself from bad weather and bites from wolves. This is a large dog, standing over 27.5 inches at the shoulders. Its hairs are up to 10.6 inches long, giving it the heaviest coat of any dog.

AMERICA'S MOST POPULAR DOG BREED
FRENCH BULLDOG

According to the American Kennel Club, the French Bulldog has, for the first time in history, taken the top spot as the club's favorite dog breed. Known affectionately as the "Frenchie," this cute, playful little dog is a bulldog in miniature, right down to the wrinkled face, snub nose, and "bat" ears. In claiming the top spot, the Frenchie finally brought an end to the Labrador Retriever's reign as the country's no. 1, which lasted an incredible thirty-one years.

AMERICA'S MOST POPULAR DOGS
1. French Bulldog
2. Labrador Retriever
3. Golden Retriever
4. German Shepherd
5. Poodle
6. Bulldog
7. Rottweiler
8. Beagle
9. Dachshund
10. German Short-Haired Pointer

AMAZING ANIMALS

WORLD'S LONGEST-LIVED LAND ANIMAL
JONATHAN

Having celebrated his 190th birthday in 2022, Jonathan the tortoise is believed to be the world's longest-lived land animal. He hatched around 1832 on the Aldabra Atoll, part of the Seychelles archipelago in the Indian Ocean. Since 1882, he's been living on a distant island in another ocean—St. Helena, part of a British overseas territory in the South Atlantic—where he was presented to the governor at the time as a gift. Today, he lives on the lawn in front of Plantation House, the official residence of the governor of St. Helena, with three other giant tortoises. Jonathan puts his longevity down to a healthy diet of fresh grass and fruit.

WORLD'S SMALLEST DOG BREED
CHIHUAHUA

The Chihuahua is the world's smallest dog breed. It originated in the northern Mexican state of Chihuahua, and is probably a descendant of the Techichi, a mute companion dog of the Toltec civilization dating back to the ninth century CE. The breed today averages 5–8 inches tall and weighs 3–6 pounds, although the world's smallest dog ever, a Chihuahua by the name of Miracle Milly, was just 3.8 inches tall and weighed no more than a pound, not much bigger than a sneaker.

AMAZING ANIMALS

WORLD'S MOST POPULAR CAT BREED
RAGDOLL

In 2023, the Cat Fanciers' Association announced that the Ragdoll was the world's most popular cat breed. This was the fourth year running that the "Raggie" had taken the top spot as the most registered cat breed of the previous year. With its lush, silky fur and big blue eyes, this is a cat that loves to be around human beings, relaxing like a "rag doll" when curled up on your lap. The year's listings also saw a newcomer claiming the no. 10 spot—the Siberian, a Russian breed that was first introduced to the United States in 1990.

WORLD'S MOST POPULAR CATS
1. Ragdoll
2. Maine Coon Cat
3. Devon Rex
4. Exotic Shorthair
5. Persian
6. British Shorthair
7. Abyssinian
8. Scottish Fold
9. Sphynx
10. Siberian

WORLD'S BALDEST CAT
SPHYNX

The Sphynx breed of cats is famous for its wrinkles and the lack of a normal coat, but it is not entirely hairless. Its skin is like the softest chamois leather, but it has a thin layer of down. It behaves more like a dog than a cat, greeting owners when they come home, and is friendly to strangers. The breed originated in Canada, where a black-and-white cat gave birth to a hairless kitten called Prune in 1966. Subsequent breeding gave rise to the Sphynx.

CHAPTER 7
INCREDIBLE
EARTH

INCREDIBLE EARTH
TRENDING

HOT IN HERE
GLOBAL HEAT WAVES BRING DANGER

The central and southern United States experienced dangerously high temperatures in 2022, with more than 125 million people advised to stay home. Heat waves cause more annual deaths than any other weather event. In September, a heat dome settled over the western United States, with California cities Sacramento and Merced reaching an all-time high of 116°F. A heat dome occurs when high pressure traps extreme heat in a particular region.

SEISMIC SHOCK
DEADLY EARTHQUAKE HITS TURKEY AND SYRIA

A 7.8-magnitude earthquake caused catastrophic damage in southeastern Turkey and parts of Syria on February 6, 2023. It occurred near the Turkish city of Nurdagi in the early morning, and a 7.5-magnitude quake followed at about 10:30 a.m. near Ekinözü. The quakes destroyed roughly 164,000 buildings and killed more than 49,000 people, many of whom were trapped under the rubble. These numbers continued to rise as severe aftershocks plagued the region into late February.

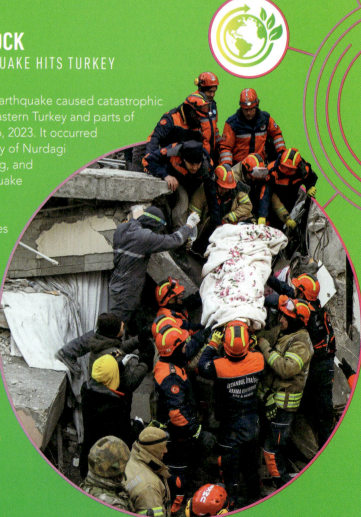

MAKING A SPLASH
TONGA VOLCANO ERUPTS

When Hunga Tonga-Hunga Ha'apai, an underwater volcano, erupted in January 2022, the nation of Tonga declared a state of emergency. Eighty-four percent of the population of the islands of Tongatapu, Ha'apai, and 'Eua were affected by tsunamis and ashfall. The eruption sent a plume of water up into the stratosphere, increasing its water vapor levels by 10 percent—an amount that could seriously impact global warming.

COLD SNAP
WINTER STORMS HIT THE UNITED STATES

December 2022 brought a dangerous winter storm to the United States, cutting power for around 700,000 people as temperatures plummeted to record lows. Winter Storm Elliott took the lives of at least sixty-nine people, dropped huge amounts of snow, and overwhelmed local power grids. One of the worst chills was in Bowman, North Dakota, where it reached −62°F over the Christmas holiday—the coldest in two decades.

PROTECTION PACT
HISTORIC DEAL MADE AT COP 15

In a huge win for biodiversity, government officials from around the world made a new agreement at the UN Biodiversity Conference (COP 15) in December 2022 to protect our natural world and transform our relationship with nature. Summit participants agreed to a global biodiversity framework that includes commitments to funding sustainable projects, addressing overexploitation and pollution, and also recognizing the rights of Indigenous peoples whose practices are tied to the land.

INCREDIBLE EARTH

OLDEST TREE ON EARTH
BRISTLECONE PINE

An unnamed bristlecone pine in the White Mountains of California is the world's oldest continuously standing tree. It is 5,070 years old, beating its bristlecone rivals the Methuselah (4,864 years old) and Prometheus (4,852 years old). Sweden is home to an even older tree, a Norway spruce (often used as Christmas trees) that took root about 9,554 years ago. However, this tree has not been standing continuously. It is long-lived because it can clone itself. When the trunk dies, a new one grows up from the same rootstock. In theory, it could live forever.

WORLD'S TALLEST TREE
CALIFORNIA REDWOOD

A coast redwood named Hyperion is the world's tallest known living tree. It is 379.1 feet tall, and could have grown taller if a woodpecker had not hammered its top. It's growing in a remote part of the Redwood National and State Parks in Northern California, but its exact location is kept a secret for fear that too many visitors would upset its ecosystem. It is thought to be 700 to 800 years old.

WORLD'S TALLEST TREES
Height in feet

Tree	Height
California redwood, California, US	379.1
Mountain ash, Styx Valley, Tasmania	327.4
Coast Douglas-fir, Oregon, US	327.3
Sitka spruce, California, US	317.0
Giant sequoia, California, US	314.0

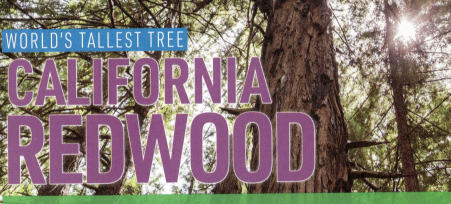

INCREDIBLE EARTH

LARGEST AND HEAVIEST FRUIT
PUMPKIN

The world's largest and heaviest fruit was a cultivated pumpkin weighing 2,625 pounds. It was grown by Belgian gardener Mathias Willemijns and certified in 2016 at the Giant Pumpkin European Championship in Germany. It's only the second time since 1900 that the title holder was not from North America. The seeds of most giant pumpkins trace their ancestry back to the Mammoth varieties of squash cultivated by Canadian pumpkin breeder Howard Dill in the 1980s.

WORLD'S TOUGHEST LEAF
GIANT AMAZON WATER LILY

The leaf of the giant Amazon water lily can grow as wide as 8.6 feet across. It has an upturned rim and a waxy, water-repellent upper surface. On the underside of the leaf is a riblike structure that traps air, enabling the leaf to float easily. The ribs are also lined with sharp spines that protect them from aquatic plant eaters. A full-grown leaf is so large and so strong that it can support up to 99 pounds in weight.

THE WORLD'S LARGEST CAVE
HANG SON DOONG
VIETNAM

Measuring 1.35 billion cubic feet, Hang Son Doong, in Vietnam, is the world's largest cave by volume. It was first discovered in 1991 by an elderly man collecting firewood, and he later revealed its location to a British caving expedition. When the explorers lit up the cave with their powerful lamps, they discovered caverns of immense size. In one, a jumbo jet could sit comfortably on the floor, with room to spare, and you could have fit in a tall skyscraper, too. The explorers went on to discover the world's tallest stalagmites—up to 250 feet tall—and a 300-foot-high calcite wall, which they nicknamed the "Great Wall of Vietnam."

GARDEN OF EDAM

At two points in the vast cave system, explorers found that the roof had collapsed and light spilled in, forming a huge circular hole called a "doline." The largest of the two dolines, the Garden of Edam, features a tropical rain forest in the center of the cave, with some trees 100 feet tall and inhabitants that include lizards, birds, and monkeys.

HANG SON DOONG STATS

Mountain river cave NAME'S MEANING

1991 YEAR OF DISCOVERY

5.6 miles TOTAL LENGTH

1.35 billion cubic feet TOTAL VOLUME

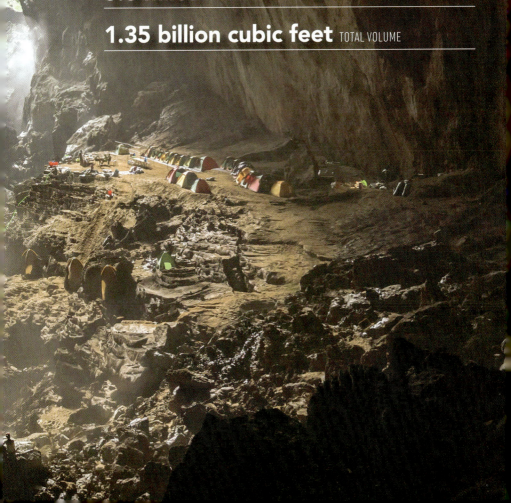

INCREDIBLE EARTH

THE DEEPEST POINT ON LAND

DENMAN GLACIER

The deepest point on land has been discovered under the Denman Glacier in East Antarctica. Deep below the Antarctic ice sheet, which is 1.3 miles thick, on average, there is an ice-filled canyon whose floor is 11,500 feet below sea level. By comparison, the lowest clearly visible point on land is in the Jordan Rift Valley, on the shore of the Dead Sea, just 1,412 feet below sea level. It makes the Denman canyon the deepest canyon on land. Only trenches at the bottom of the ocean are deeper. The floor of the deepest trench—the Mariana Trench—is close to 7 miles below the sea's surface.

WORLD'S GREATEST NUMBER OF GEYSERS
YELLOWSTONE NATIONAL PARK

There are about 1,000 geysers that erupt worldwide, and 540 of them are in Yellowstone National Park, US. That's the greatest concentration of geysers on Earth. The most famous is Old Faithful, which spews out a cloud of steam and hot water to a maximum height of 185 feet every 44 to 125 minutes. Yellowstone's spectacular water display is due to its closeness to molten rock from Earth's mantle that rises up to the surface. One day the park could face an eruption 1,000 times as powerful as that of Mount St. Helens in 1980.

GEYSER FIELDS
Number of geysers

- **Yellowstone**, Idaho/Montana/Wyoming, US **540**
- **Valley of Geysers**, Kamchatka, Russia **139**
- **El Tatio**, Andes, Chile **84**
- **Orakei Korako**, New Zealand **33**
- **Hveravellir**, Iceland **16**

INCREDIBLE EARTH

EARTH'S TALLEST MOUNTAIN ABOVE SEA LEVEL

MOUNT EVEREST

Mount Everest has grown. In December 2020, Nepal and China agreed on an official height that is 2.8 feet higher than the previous calculation. The mega mountain is located in the Himalayas, on the border between Tibet and Nepal. The mountain acquired its official name from surveyor Sir George Everest, but local people know it as Chomolungma (Tibet) or Sagarmatha (Nepal). In 1953, Sir Edmund Hillary and Tenzing Norgay were the first people to reach its summit. Now more than 650 people per year manage to make the spectacular climb.

WORLD'S TALLEST MOUNTAINS
Height above sea level in feet

- K2 (Qogir), Pakistan/China — 28,251
- Everest, Tibet — 29,032
- Kanchenjunga, India/Nepal — 28,179
- Makalu, Tibet/Nepal — 27,838
- Lhotse, Tibet/Nepal — 27,940

168

GREAT BARRIER REEF

WORLD'S LONGEST CORAL REEF SYSTEM

Australia's Great Barrier Reef is the only living thing that's clearly visible from space. It stretches along the Queensland coast for 1,400 miles, making it the largest coral reef system in the world. At its northern tip, scientists have discovered a towering, blade-shaped reef, taller than the Empire State Building, that is a mile wide at its base and tapers to a knife edge about 130 feet below the surface. In recent years, climate change has posed a huge threat to the world's coral reefs, with rising sea temperatures causing areas to die off. The northern half of the Great Barrier Reef suffered particularly in 2016, and scientists fear that more damage is yet to come.

WORLD'S LONGEST CORAL REEFS
Length in miles

- Great Barrier Reef, Australia **1,400**
- New Caledonia Barrier Reef, South Pacific **930**
- Mesoamerican Barrier Reef, Caribbean **620**
- Ningaloo Reef, Western Australia **162**

INCREDIBLE EARTH

WORLD'S LARGEST HOT DESERT
SAHARA DESERT

WORLD'S LARGEST HOT DESERTS
Size in square miles

- **Sahara Desert**, North Africa
- **Arabian Desert**, Western Asia
- **Great Victoria Desert**, Australia
- **Kalahari Desert**, Africa
- **Syrian Desert**, Western Asia

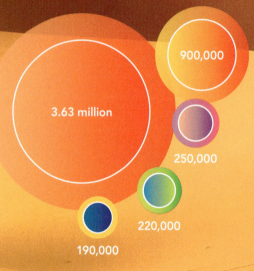

- 3.63 million
- 900,000
- 250,000
- 220,000
- 190,000

Sahara means simply "great desert," and great it is. It's the largest hot desert on the planet. It's almost the same size as the United States or China and dominates North Africa from the Atlantic Ocean in the west to the Red Sea in the east. This desert is extremely dry, with most of the Sahara receiving less than 0.1 inch of rain a year, and some places get none at all for several years. It is stiflingly hot, up to 122°F, making this one of the hottest and driest regions in the world.

WORLD'S LARGEST LAKE
CASPIAN SEA

- 31,700
- 149,200
- 26,600
- 22,300
- 23,000

WORLD'S LARGEST LAKES
Area in square miles

- **Caspian Sea**, Europe/Asia
- **Lake Superior**, North America
- **Lake Victoria**, Africa
- **Lake Huron**, North America
- **Lake Michigan**, North America

The countries of Russia, Kazakhstan, Turkmenistan, Iran, and Azerbaijan border the vast Caspian Sea, the largest inland body of water on Earth. Once part of an ancient sea, the lake became landlocked between five and ten million years ago, with occasional fills of salt water as sea levels fluctuated over time. Now it has a surface area of about 149,200 square miles and is home to one of the world's most valuable fish: the beluga sturgeon, the source of beluga caviar, which costs up to $2,250 per pound.

INCREDIBLE EARTH

NILE RIVER
WORLD'S LONGEST RIVER

Flowing from south to north through eastern Africa, the Nile River is the world's longest. It begins in rivers that flow into Lake Victoria, which borders modern-day Uganda, Tanzania, and Kenya. One of those rivers is the Kagera River. From the lake, the Nile proper heads north across eastern Africa for 4,132 miles to the Mediterranean. Its water is crucial to people living along its banks. They use it to irrigate precious crops, generate electricity, and, in the lower reaches, as a river highway.

WORLD'S LONGEST RIVERS
Length in miles

Nile River, Africa **4,132**

Amazon River, South America **4,000**

Yangtze River, China **3,915**

Mississippi-Missouri river system, US **3,710**

Yellow River, China **3,395**

172

NEW SURFING RECORD
NAZARÉ

The world's tallest surfable waves, some up to 80 feet tall, break on the Portuguese coast at Nazaré. It's the place where serious surfers hang out, and in February 2020, Brazilian surfer Maya Gabeira rode a wave 73.5 feet tall. It was the highest wave of the 2019–2020 winter surf season, although Gabeira almost didn't get the chance. While surfing in 2013, she was knocked unconscious by a wipeout at Nazaré, and was found facedown in the water with leg and back injuries. After three operations to mend her broken body, she survived and is now a champion!

WILDFIRES 2022

The West Coast of the United States was hit hard by wildfires in 2022. In Oregon, numerous lightning strikes in the Willamette National Forest caused the Cedar Creek Fire. About 127,311 acres of woodland were destroyed and the city of Oakridge evacuated. In California, there were close to 170 separate incidents. The biggest of the 2022 season was the Mosquito Fire in Northern California. It started during a record-breaking September heat wave when the moisture content of vegetation was at an all-time low. As of early 2023 the fire was still under investigation. It is thought that electrical equipment caused the fire, and about 76,790 acres went up in flames, including sections of the Tahoe and Eldorado National Forests. It was brought under control by nearly 3,700 firefighters about six weeks later.

SHORT ON RESOURCES

As a sign of the times, many out-of-control forest fires occurred in Siberia from spring until fall. The military, usually deployed to manage the fires, had been otherwise engaged—fighting a war in Ukraine.

MEGA-FIRES

In Europe, the Gironde Fires—described as "mega-fires"—in the South of France burned throughout the summer, destroying up to 51,000 acres of countryside and villages. Thousands of residents and vacationers were evacuated, houses and businesses were destroyed, and firefighting personnel and equipment were brought in from all over Europe. These mega-fires occurred when the July air temperature in the region peaked at 108.3°F, and with no rain, it was the driest July since records for the region began.

INCREDIBLE EARTH

WORLD'S LARGEST PERMAFROST CRATER
BATAGAIKA CRATER
SIBERIA

There is a huge gash in the permafrost of Siberia. Local people know it as the "gateway to the underworld," but to Russian geologists it is the Batagaika Crater, the largest permafrost crater in the world. At nearly 2 miles long and half a mile across at the widest point, the crater is visible from space. It has appeared because the permafrost—normally permanently frozen soil—is thawing. The effects of climate change are causing the ice that keeps the soil solid to melt, and the meltwater is washing the soil away, forming "slumps." Categorized as a mega-slump, Batagaika Crater is enlarging at a rate of about 100 feet per year.

LONGEST LIGHTNING FLASH
UNITED STATES

In February 2022, the World Meteorological Organization (WMO) announced a new record for the world's longest single lightning flash, which it had discovered by scanning satellite imagery. The strike occurred two years earlier, on April 29, 2020. In the event, a 477.2-mile-long megaflash of lightning ripped through the skies above Mississippi, Louisiana, and Texas—quite a record, given that strikes rarely stretch over 10 miles. The megaflash was just 36 miles longer than the previous record holder, a 440.6-mile-long strike in Brazil on October 31, 2018.

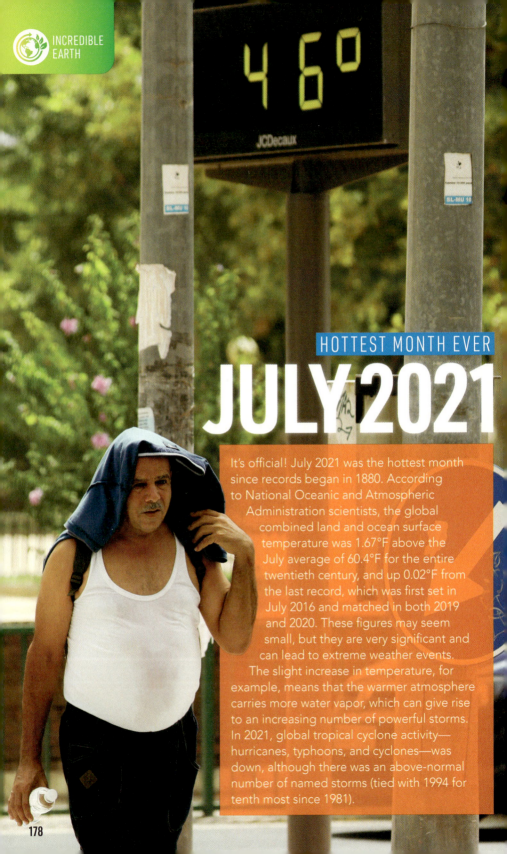

INCREDIBLE EARTH

HOTTEST MONTH EVER
JULY 2021

It's official! July 2021 was the hottest month since records began in 1880. According to National Oceanic and Atmospheric Administration scientists, the global combined land and ocean surface temperature was 1.67°F above the July average of 60.4°F for the entire twentieth century, and up 0.02°F from the last record, which was first set in July 2016 and matched in both 2019 and 2020. These figures may seem small, but they are very significant and can lead to extreme weather events.

The slight increase in temperature, for example, means that the warmer atmosphere carries more water vapor, which can give rise to an increasing number of powerful storms. In 2021, global tropical cyclone activity—hurricanes, typhoons, and cyclones—was down, although there was an above-normal number of named storms (tied with 1994 for tenth most since 1981).

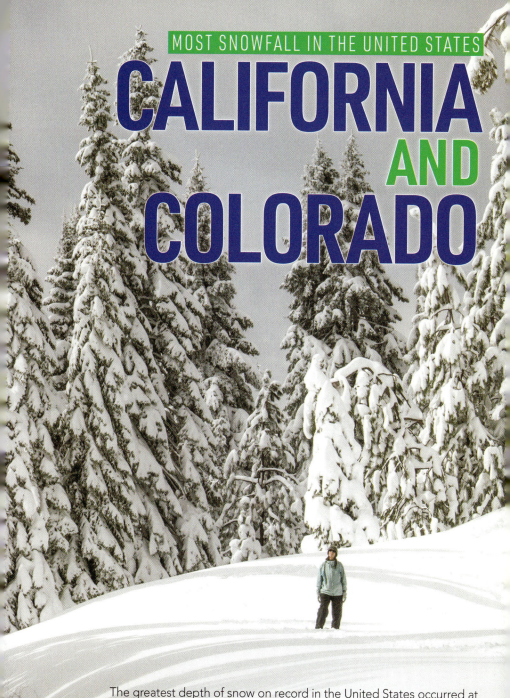

MOST SNOWFALL IN THE UNITED STATES
CALIFORNIA AND COLORADO

The greatest depth of snow on record in the United States occurred at Tamarack, near the Bear Valley ski resort in California, on March 11, 1911. The snow reached an incredible 37.8 feet deep. Tamarack also holds the record for the most snowfall in a single month, with 32.5 feet in January 1911. Mount Shasta, California, had the most snowfall in a single storm, with 15.75 feet falling during February 13–19, 1959. The most snow in twenty-four hours was a snowfall of 6.3 feet at Silver Lake, Colorado, on April 14–15, 1921.

INCREDIBLE EARTH

WORLD'S LARGEST HAILSTONE

SOUTH DAKOTA

In August 2010, the town of Vivian, South Dakota, was bombarded by some of the biggest hailstones ever to have fallen out of the sky. They went straight through roofs of houses, smashed car windshields, and stripped vegetation. Among them was a world record breaker, a hailstone the size of a volleyball. It was 8 inches in diameter and weighed 2.2 pounds.

WORLD'S WETTEST PLACE
MAWSYNRAM

Mawsynram is a cluster of villages in the Khasi Hills of India. The plateau on which they sit overlooks the vast flatlands of Bangladesh. With 467.4 inches of rain falling each year, on average, Mawsynram is considered to be the wettest place on Earth. Life here is not without its problems. Wooden bridges are washed away frequently, so locals build living bridges of knotted and interwoven roots of Indian rubber trees. Some people use a traditional "knup" umbrella in the heavy rains. Woven from reeds, this keeps the whole body dry.

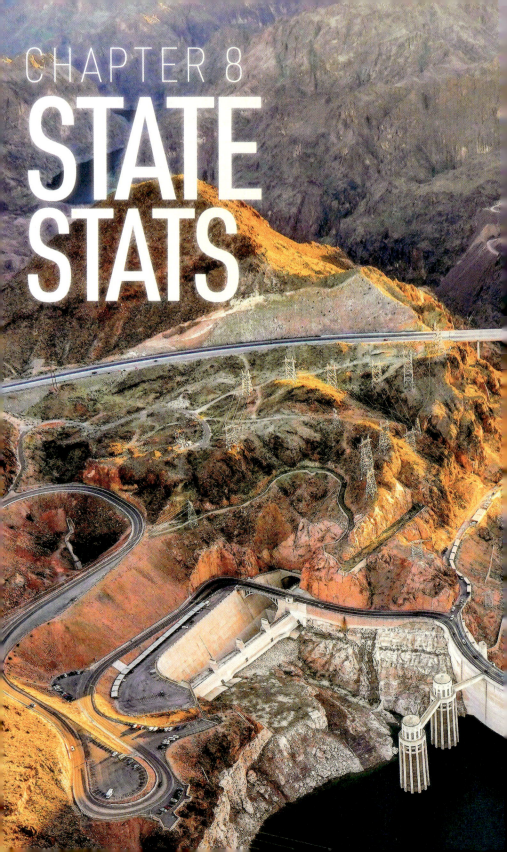

CHAPTER 8
STATE STATS

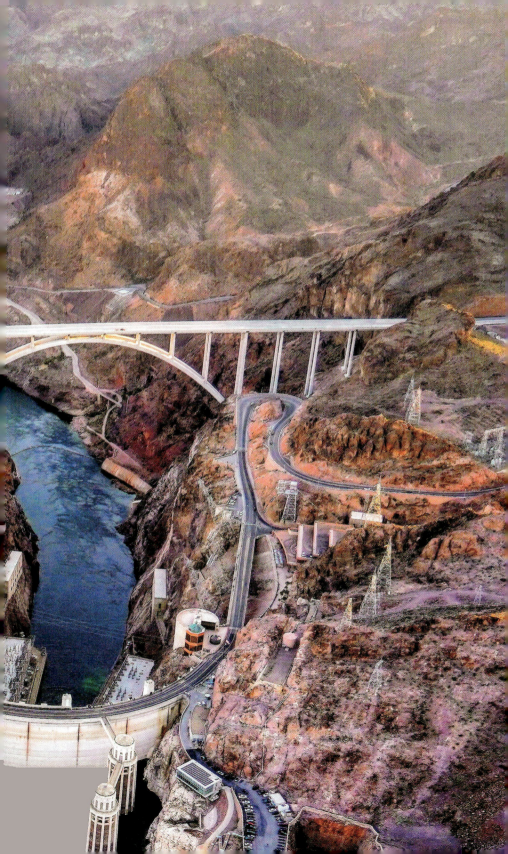

STATE STATS
TRENDING

DOING THE WORM
HEIDI KLUM'S HILARIOUS HALLOWEEN LOOK

Supermodel Heidi Klum is known for the outrageous costumes she showcases at her annual Halloween party. In 2022, she outdid herself by appearing in her strangest outfit yet—as a worm! Red-carpet snaps from the event show Klum lying on the ground in a super-realistic foam-and-latex creation, in which only her eyes and mouth were visible. Klum was trapped inside the costume and described her dancing that night as "worming around."

100 YEARS OF MAGIC
DISNEY SUPER BOWL AD CELEBRATES ANNIVERSARY

The most effective Super Bowl ad of 2023 was Disney's first major celebration of a century of storytelling, with its "Disney100 Special Look." The ad was jam-packed with clips, from 1928's *Steamboat Willie*—the official debut of Minnie and Mickey Mouse—to modern Disney acquisitions like *Star Wars*. The ad also featured a voiceover from Walt Disney himself, as well as fan videos to thank viewers for making Disney's dreams come true. Disney Brothers Cartoon Studio was founded by Walt and his brother Roy on October 16, 1923.

184

ALL CHANGE
MIDTERMS SHAKE THINGS UP

The midterm elections in November 2022 signaled the end of an era for Nancy Pelosi, whose tenure as the first female speaker in the US House of Representatives came to a close. However, it also ushered in a new first: Hakeem Jeffries stepped into Pelosi's impressive shoes, becoming the first Black party leader in US history. Jeffries, a lawmaker from New York, was elected by the Democrats in November to lead the party and became minority leader after the midterms flipped control of the House to the Republicans.

#PINKSAUCE
COLORFUL CONDIMENT ON SALE

Created by TikTok star Chef Pii, Pink Sauce became an Internet sensation in 2022. The product was launched to a huge amount of fanfare, but things soon turned sour when Chef Pii came under fire for not getting the sauce approved by the FDA. The story had a happy ending, however, after Chef Pii partnered with Dave's Gourmet, securing a deal for a reformulated version of the sauce to be sold in Walmart.

CLAMTASTIC
RETURN OF AN INDIGENOUS GARDEN

Members of the Swinomish community gathered in Washington State in August 2022 to build their first clam garden in centuries. Clam gardens are an ancient practice used by Indigenous peoples to cultivate shellfish, but a new one had not been built for around 200 years. The Swinomish clam garden was created by building a 2-foot-high, 200-foot-long wall on the shore at the Kukutali Preserve. People passed individual rocks from hand to hand to build it, making it a true community effort.

USA STATE STATS

STATE WITH THE OLDEST MARDI GRAS CELEBRATION
ALABAMA

French settlers held the first American Mardi Gras in Mobile, Alabama, in 1703. Yearly celebrations continued until the Civil War and began again in 1866. Today, 800,000 people gather in the city during the vibrant two-week festival. Dozens of parades with colorful floats and marching bands wind through the streets each day. Partygoers attend masked balls and other lively events sponsored by the city's social societies. On Mardi Gras, which means "Fat Tuesday" in French, six parades continue the party until the stroke of midnight, which marks the end of the year's festivities and the beginning of Lent.

STATE WITH THE MOST NATIVE AMERICANS PER CAPITA
ALASKA

With a total population of 725,000 people and a Native American population exceeding 145,000, Alaska is the state with the highest number of Native Americans per capita—approximately one in five. Alaska is also the state with the highest number of tribal areas, having more than 200 Native villages in total. Among the great Indigenous tribes of Alaska are the Aleut, the Yup'ik, the Eyak, and the Inuit. While most live in modern communities, each tribe continues to uphold the traditions of its elders.

USA STATE STATS

LARGEST DAM IN THE US
ARIZONA

The state of Arizona is home to the nation's largest dam by volume, an honor it shares with Nevada, since the dam straddles the state border. Finished in 1935, the Hoover Dam was a massive feat of engineering that took around 21,000 people to build; it stands at an amazing 726.4 feet from the rocky bottom to the road over the top. The Hoover Dam is a concrete arch-gravity dam, which means it controls the movement of the water both through its arch shape, pointing upstream, and the use of gravity. The dam not only controls the flow of the mighty Colorado River, but also generates a huge amount of hydroelectric power as it does so—enough for more than 1.3 million people.

ONLY STATE WHERE DIAMONDS ARE MINED
ARKANSAS

Crater of Diamonds, near Murfreesboro, Arkansas, is the only active public diamond mine in the United States. Farmer and former owner John Wesley Huddleston first discovered diamonds there in August 1906, and a diamond rush overwhelmed the area after he sold the property to a mining company. For a time, there were two competing mines in this area, but in 1969 General Earth Minerals bought both mines to run them as private tourist attractions. Since 1972, the land has been owned by the state of Arkansas, which designated the area as Crater of Diamonds State Park. Visitors can pay a fee to search through plowed fields in the hope of discovering a gem for themselves.

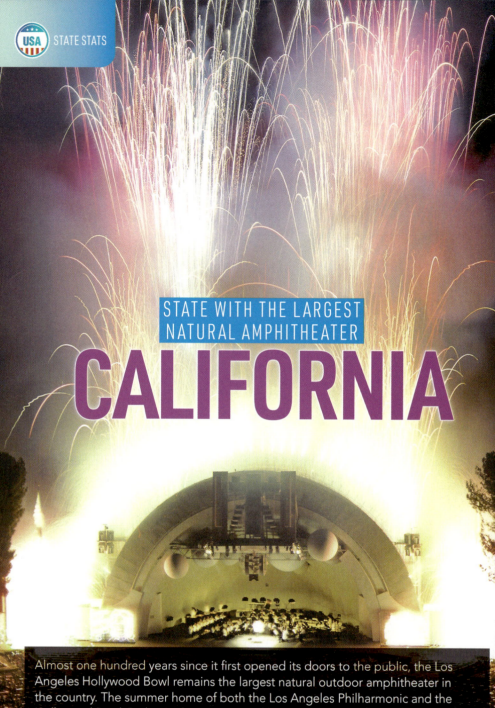

USA STATE STATS

STATE WITH THE LARGEST NATURAL AMPHITHEATER

CALIFORNIA

Almost one hundred years since it first opened its doors to the public, the Los Angeles Hollywood Bowl remains the largest natural outdoor amphitheater in the country. The summer home of both the Los Angeles Philharmonic and the Hollywood Bowl Orchestra has a capacity for approximately 17,000 people. Many bring picnics and blankets to make the most of their music-filled summer evenings under the stars. Several events have drawn record crowds, including The Beatles, who attracted 18,700 fans in 1964, and Chris Tomlin, whose 2019 performance was a sellout. The highest attendance record of all time goes to the French singer Lily Pons, whose 1936 performance drew an incredible 26,410 people.

STATE WITH THE LARGEST ELK POPULATION
COLORADO

Colorado is currently home to around 280,000 elk, making it the state with the largest elk population. Elk live on both public and private land across the state, from the mountainous regions to lower terrain. Popular targets for hunting, these creatures are regulated by both the Colorado Parks and Wildlife department and the National Park Service. Many elk live within the boundaries of Colorado's Rocky Mountain National Park. Elk are among the largest members of the deer family, and the males—called bulls—are distinguishable by their majestic antlers.

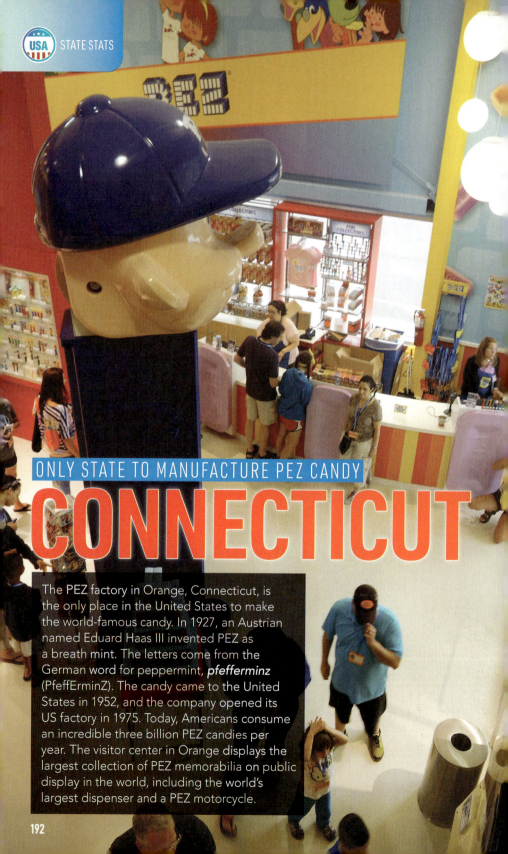

USA STATE STATS

ONLY STATE TO MANUFACTURE PEZ CANDY
CONNECTICUT

The PEZ factory in Orange, Connecticut, is the only place in the United States to make the world-famous candy. In 1927, an Austrian named Eduard Haas III invented PEZ as a breath mint. The letters come from the German word for peppermint, *pfefferminz* (PfeffErminZ). The candy came to the United States in 1952, and the company opened its US factory in 1975. Today, Americans consume an incredible three billion PEZ candies per year. The visitor center in Orange displays the largest collection of PEZ memorabilia on public display in the world, including the world's largest dispenser and a PEZ motorcycle.

STATE WITH THE MOST HORSESHOE CRABS
DELAWARE

Delaware Bay has the largest American horseshoe crab (*Limulus polyphemus*) population in the world. These creatures can be seen in large numbers on the bay's beaches in the spring. They appear during high tides on new and full moons, when they come onto land to spawn (deposit eggs). Horseshoe crabs have changed very little in the past 250 million years and have, therefore, been called "living fossils." It is impossible to know the exact number of horseshoe crabs in the region, so every spring, volunteers at some of the state's beaches conduct counts to track spawning activity. Results from the most recent survey, published in 2021 by the Delaware Center for the Inland Bays, recorded an estimated seasonal count of 1,846,490 horseshoe crabs on its beaches.

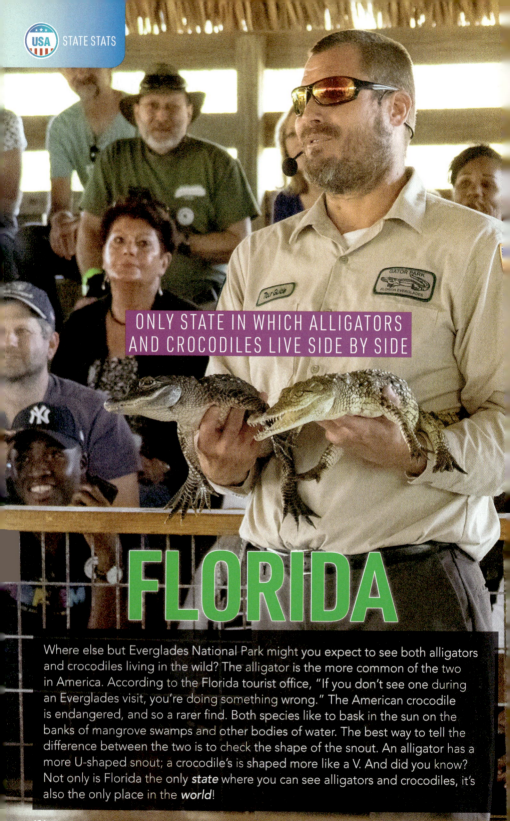

USA STATE STATS

ONLY STATE IN WHICH ALLIGATORS AND CROCODILES LIVE SIDE BY SIDE

FLORIDA

Where else but Everglades National Park might you expect to see both alligators and crocodiles living in the wild? The alligator is the more common of the two in America. According to the Florida tourist office, "If you don't see one during an Everglades visit, you're doing something wrong." The American crocodile is endangered, and so a rarer find. Both species like to bask in the sun on the banks of mangrove swamps and other bodies of water. The best way to tell the difference between the two is to check the shape of the snout. An alligator has a more U-shaped snout; a crocodile's is shaped more like a V. And did you know? Not only is Florida the only *state* where you can see alligators and crocodiles, it's also the only place in the *world*!

STATE WITH THE LARGEST SPORTS HALL OF FAME

GEORGIA

At 43,000 square feet, Georgia's Sports Hall of Fame honors the state's greatest sports stars and coaches. The museum includes 14,000 square feet of exhibition space and a 205-seat theater. It owns more than 3,000 artifacts and memorabilia from Georgia's professional, college, and amateur athletes. At least 1,000 of these artifacts are on display at any time. The Hall of Fame corridor features over 400 inductees, such as golf legend Bobby Jones, baseball hero Jackie Robinson, and Olympic track medalist Wyomia Tyus.

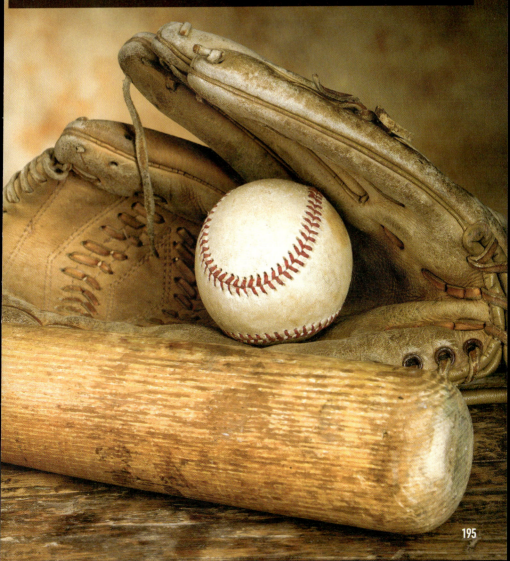

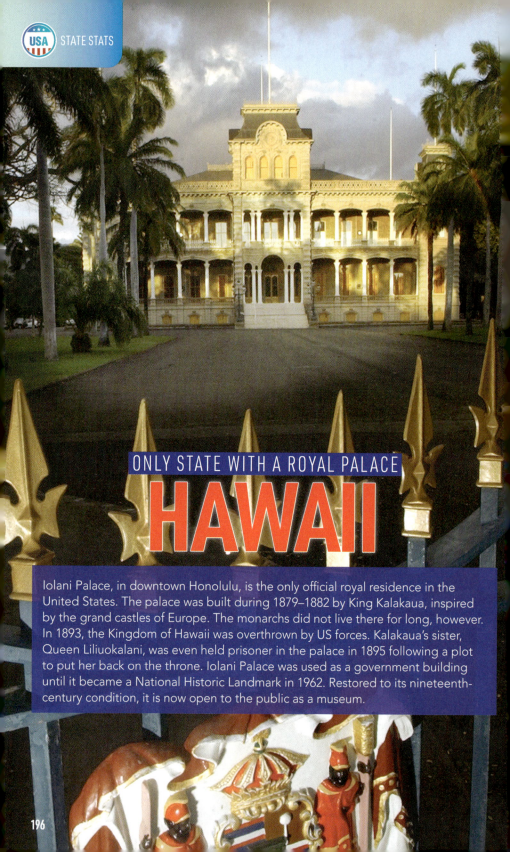

USA STATE STATS

ONLY STATE WITH A ROYAL PALACE
HAWAII

Iolani Palace, in downtown Honolulu, is the only official royal residence in the United States. The palace was built during 1879–1882 by King Kalakaua, inspired by the grand castles of Europe. The monarchs did not live there for long, however. In 1893, the Kingdom of Hawaii was overthrown by US forces. Kalakaua's sister, Queen Liliuokalani, was even held prisoner in the palace in 1895 following a plot to put her back on the throne. Iolani Palace was used as a government building until it became a National Historic Landmark in 1962. Restored to its nineteenth-century condition, it is now open to the public as a museum.

FIRST STATE WITH A BLUE FOOTBALL FIELD
IDAHO

Boise State's Albertsons Stadium, originally dubbed the "Smurf Turf" and now nicknamed "The Blue," was the first blue football field in the United States. In 1986, when the time came to upgrade the old turf, athletics director Gene Bleymaier realized that they would be spending a lot of money on the new field, yet most spectators wouldn't notice the difference. So he asked AstroTurf to create the new field in the school's colors. Since the field's creation, students at the school have consistently voted for blue turf each time the field has been upgraded. Today, nine teams play on a colored playing field, including the Coastal Carolina Chanticleers, whose teal field is dubbed the "Surf Turf."

USA STATE STATS

STATE WITH THE OLDEST FREE PUBLIC ZOO

ILLINOIS

Lincoln Park Zoo, in Chicago, Illinois, remains the oldest free public zoo in the United States. Founded in 1868—just nine years after the Philadelphia Zoo, the country's oldest zoo overall—Lincoln Park Zoo does not charge admission fees. More than two-thirds of the money for the zoo's operating budget comes from food, retail, parking, and fundraisers. Nonetheless, the zoo continues to grow. In November 2016, it opened a new exhibit—the Walter Family Arctic Tundra—to house its newest addition: a seven-year-old male polar bear named Siku.

THE FIRST PROFESSIONAL BASEBALL GAME
INDIANA

On May 4, 1871, the first National Association professional baseball game took place on Hamilton Field in Fort Wayne, Indiana. The home team, the Kekiongas, took on the Forest Citys of Cleveland, beating them 2–0 against the odds. The Kekiongas were a little-known team at the time. In fact, the first professional game had been scheduled to take place between two better-known teams, the Washington Olympics and the Cincinnati Red Stockings in Washington, DC, on May 3. Heavy rain forced a cancellation, however, and so history was made at Fort Wayne the following day.

USA STATE STATS

STATE WITH THE SHORTEST, STEEPEST RAILROAD

IOWA

At only 296 feet long, Fenelon Place Elevator in Dubuque, Iowa, is the shortest railroad in the United States, and its elevation of 189 feet also makes it the steepest. The original railway was built in 1882 by businessman and former mayor J. K. Graves, who lived at the top of the Mississippi River bluff and wanted a quicker commute down into the town below. Today's railway, modernized in 1977, is open to the public. It costs $2 for an adult one-way trip and consists of two house-shaped cars traveling in opposite directions on parallel tracks.

LARGEST TALLGRASS PRAIRIE
KANSAS

At just 60 miles wide, Flint Hills, Kansas's Tallgrass Prairie National Preserve, is the only US national park dedicated to this ecosystem. Due to plowing by farmers who use the fertile ground to plant crops, the ecosystem is in danger of disappearing worldwide. It has survived in Flint Hills partly because the landscape is not suitable for plowing. The tallgrass prairie contains more than 500 plant species, including different types of grass—notably Indian grass and big bluestem. In 2009, bison were reintroduced to the preserve in Kansas, and the herd has since grown to about 100 strong.

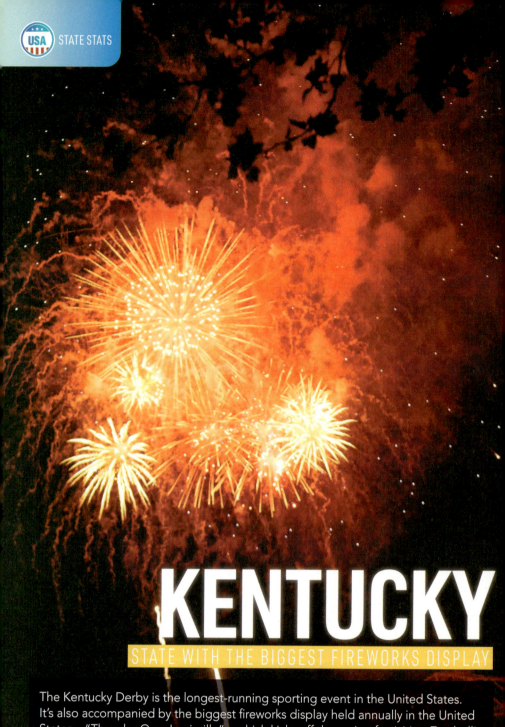

USA STATE STATS

KENTUCKY
STATE WITH THE BIGGEST FIREWORKS DISPLAY

The Kentucky Derby is the longest-running sporting event in the United States. It's also accompanied by the biggest fireworks display held annually in the United States—"Thunder Over Louisville"—which kicks off the racing festivities. Zambelli Fireworks, the display's creator, says that the show requires nearly 60 tons of fireworks shells and a massive 700 miles of wire cable to sync the fireworks to music. The theme for the 2023 show was "Through the Decades," a fabulous celebration of the most memorable Thunder moments over the years.

STATE WITH THE MOST CRAWFISH
LOUISIANA

The majority of the crawfish consumed in the United States are caught in the state of Louisiana. While these critters may look like tiny lobsters, crawfish are actually freshwater shellfish and are abundant in the mud of the state's bayous—sometimes they are called "mudbugs." Before white settlers arrived in Louisiana, crawfish were a favorite food of the Native tribes, who caught them using reeds baited with venison. Today, crawfish are both commercially farmed and caught in their natural habitat. The industry currently yields more than 100 million pounds of crawfish a year, and the crustaceans are an integral part of the state's culture, with backyard crawfish boils remaining a popular local tradition.

USA STATE STATS

STATE WITH THE OLDEST STATE FAIR

MAINE

In January 1819, the Somerset Central Agricultural Society sponsored the first-ever Skowhegan State Fair. In the 1800s, state fairs were important places for farmers to gather and learn about new agricultural methods and equipment. After Maine became a state in 1820, the fair continued to grow in size and popularity, gaining its official name in 1842. Today, the Skowhegan State Fair welcomes more than 7,000 exhibitors and 100,000 visitors. Enthusiasts can watch events that include livestock competitions, tractor pulling, a demolition derby, and much more during the ten-day show.

STATE WITH THE OLDEST CAPITOL BUILDING
MARYLAND

The Maryland State House in Annapolis is both the oldest capitol building in continuous legislative use and the only statehouse to have once been used as the national capitol. The Continental Congress met there from 1783 to 1784, and it was where George Washington formally resigned as commander in chief of the army following the American Revolution. The current building is the third to be erected on that site and was actually incomplete when the Continental Congress met there in 1783, despite the cornerstone being laid in 1772. The interior of the building was finished in 1797, but not without tragedy—plasterer Thomas Dance fell to his death while working on the dome in 1793.

OLDEST CAPITOL BUILDINGS IN 2023
Age of building (year work was started)

1722
Maryland
251 years

1785
Virginia
238 years

1792
New Jersey
231 years

1795
Massachusetts
228 years

1816
New Hampshire
207 years

USA STATE STATS

STATE WITH THE OLDEST THANKSGIVING CELEBRATION

MASSACHUSETTS

The first Thanksgiving celebration took place in 1621, in Plymouth, Massachusetts, when the Pilgrims and the Native Wampanoag people shared a feast. While the celebration became widespread in the Northeast in the late-seventeenth century, Thanksgiving was not celebrated nationally until 1863, when magazine editor Sarah Josepha Hale's writings convinced President Abraham Lincoln to make it a national holiday. Today, Plymouth, Massachusetts, holds a weekend-long celebration honoring its history: the America's Hometown Thanksgiving Celebration.

STATE WITH THE MOST LIGHTHOUSES

MICHIGAN

Michigan is home to more than 120 lighthouses! This is hardly surprising, given that Michigan is surrounded by four of the five Great Lakes and has about 3,288 miles of coastline. As many as 1,500 lighthouses were built in the United States—most of them in the early twentieth century. They are somewhat redundant today, because modern lighthouses now use technology to safely guide boats into harbors at night. But without these old lighthouses, many ships would have scuppered on the craggy rocks.

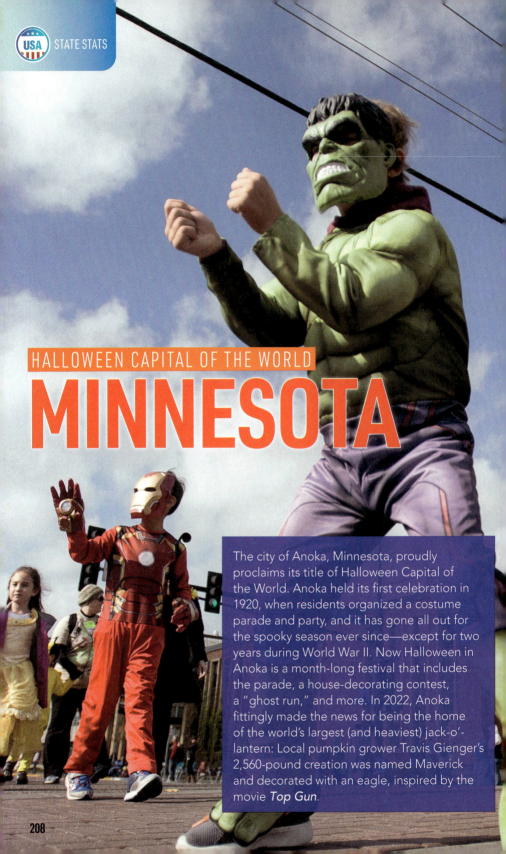

USA STATE STATS

HALLOWEEN CAPITAL OF THE WORLD
MINNESOTA

The city of Anoka, Minnesota, proudly proclaims its title of Halloween Capital of the World. Anoka held its first celebration in 1920, when residents organized a costume parade and party, and it has gone all out for the spooky season ever since—except for two years during World War II. Now Halloween in Anoka is a month-long festival that includes the parade, a house-decorating contest, a "ghost run," and more. In 2022, Anoka fittingly made the news for being the home of the world's largest (and heaviest) jack-o'-lantern: Local pumpkin grower Travis Gienger's 2,560-pound creation was named Maverick and decorated with an eagle, inspired by the movie *Top Gun*.

ONLY STATE TO HOLD THE INTERNATIONAL BALLET COMPETITION

MISSISSIPPI

Every four years, Jackson, Mississippi, hosts the USA International Ballet Competition, a two-week Olympic-style event that awards gold, silver, and bronze medals. The most recent one was held here in 2023. The competition began in 1964 in Varna, Bulgaria, and rotated among the cities of Varna; Moscow, Russia; and Tokyo, Japan. In June 1979, the competition came to the United States for the first time, and in 1982 Congress passed a joint resolution designating Jackson as the official home of the competition. Dancers vie for prizes and a chance to join ballet companies.

USA STATE STATS

It is said that America's first ice cream cone was introduced through chance inspiration at the St. Louis World's Fair in 1904. According to the most popular story, a Syrian salesman named Ernest Hamwi saw that an ice-cream vendor had plenty of ice cream but not enough cups and spoons to serve it. Seeing that a neighboring vendor was selling waffle cookies, Hamwi took a cookie and rolled it into a cone for holding ice cream. An immediate success, Hamwi's invention was hailed by vendors as a "cornucopia"—an exotic word for a "cone."

AMERICA'S FIRST ICE CREAM CONE

MISSOURI

STATE WITH THE MOST *T. REX* SPECIMENS
MONTANA

The first *Tyrannosaurus rex* fossil ever found was discovered in Montana—paleontologist Barnum Brown excavated it in the Hell Creek Formation in 1902. Since then, many major **T. rex** finds have been made in Montana—from the "Wankel Rex," discovered in 1988, to "Trix," unearthed in 2013, and "Tufts-Love Rex," discovered in 2016. This last was found about 20 percent intact at the site in the Hell Creek Formation. In recent years, a new exhibit named "Dinosaurs Under the Big Sky" has been installed in the Siebel Dinosaur Complex at the Museum of the Rockies in Bozeman, Montana. It is one of the largest and most up-to-date dinosaur exhibits in the world.

USA STATE STATS

STATE WITH THE LARGEST INDOOR RAIN FOREST

NEBRASKA

The Lied Jungle at the Henry Doorly Zoo in Omaha, Nebraska, features three rain forest habitats: one each from South America, Africa, and Asia. At 123,000 square feet, this indoor rain forest is larger than two football fields. It measures 80 feet tall, making it as tall as an eight-story building. The Lied Jungle opened in 1992 and cost $15 million to create. Seven waterfalls rank among its spectacular features. Ninety different animal species live here, including saki monkeys, pygmy hippos, and many reptiles and birds. Exotic plant life includes the African sausage tree, the chocolate tree, and rare orchids. The zoo's other major exhibit—the Desert Dome—is the world's largest indoor desert.

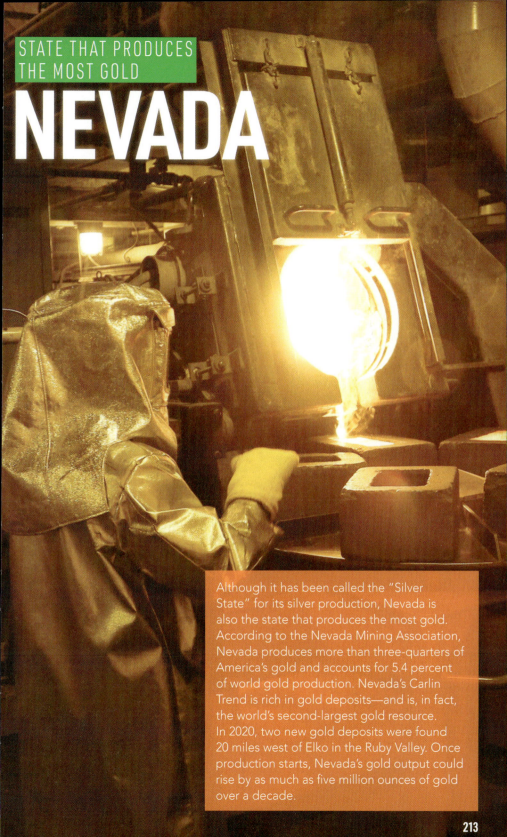

STATE THAT PRODUCES THE MOST GOLD

NEVADA

Although it has been called the "Silver State" for its silver production, Nevada is also the state that produces the most gold. According to the Nevada Mining Association, Nevada produces more than three-quarters of America's gold and accounts for 5.4 percent of world gold production. Nevada's Carlin Trend is rich in gold deposits—and is, in fact, the world's second-largest gold resource. In 2020, two new gold deposits were found 20 miles west of Elko in the Ruby Valley. Once production starts, Nevada's gold output could rise by as much as five million ounces of gold over a decade.

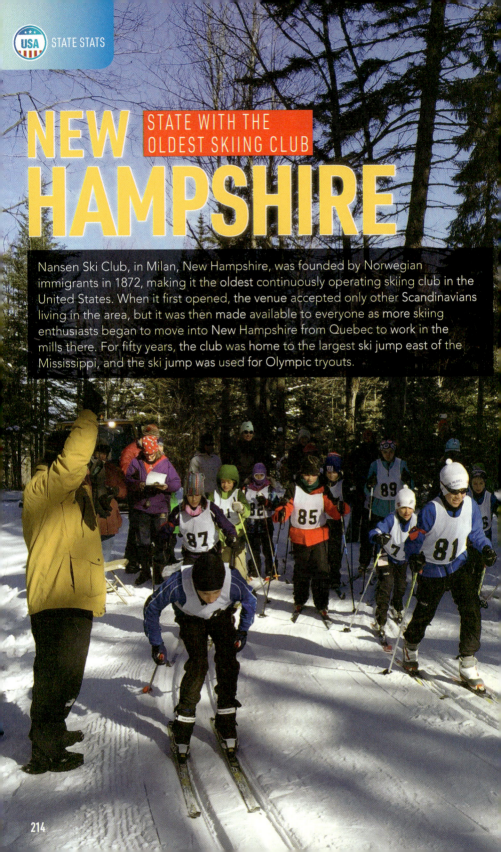

USA STATE STATS

NEW HAMPSHIRE

STATE WITH THE OLDEST SKIING CLUB

Nansen Ski Club, in Milan, New Hampshire, was founded by Norwegian immigrants in 1872, making it the oldest continuously operating skiing club in the United States. When it first opened, the venue accepted only other Scandinavians living in the area, but it was then made available to everyone as more skiing enthusiasts began to move into New Hampshire from Quebec to work in the mills there. For fifty years, the club was home to the largest ski jump east of the Mississippi, and the ski jump was used for Olympic tryouts.

STATE WITH THE MOST DINERS

NEW JERSEY

The state of New Jersey has more than six hundred diners, earning it the title of "Diner Capital of the World." The state has a higher concentration of diners than anywhere else in the United States. They are such an iconic part of the state's identity that, in 2016, a New Jersey diners exhibit opened at the Middlesex County Museum, showcasing the history of the diner, from early twentieth-century lunch cars to modern roadside spots. The state has many different types of diners, including famous restaurant-style eateries like Tops in East Newark, as well as retro hole-in-the-wall diners with jukeboxes and booths.

USA STATE STATS

STATE THAT MADE THE WORLD'S LARGEST FLAT ENCHILADA

NEW MEXICO

New Mexico was home to the world's largest flat enchilada in October 2014, during the Whole Enchilada Fiesta in Las Cruces. The record-breaking enchilada measured 10.5 feet in diameter and required 250 pounds of masa dough, 175 pounds of cheese, 75 gallons of red chili sauce, 50 pounds of onions, and 175 gallons of oil. Led by Roberto's Mexican Restaurant, the making—and eating—of the giant enchilada was a tradition at the festival for thirty-four years before enchilada master Roberto Estrada retired in 2015.

AMERICA'S SMALLEST CHURCH
NEW YORK

The smallest church in America, Oneida's Cross Island Chapel, measures 81 by 51 inches and has just enough room for the minister and two churchgoers. Built in 1989, the church is in an odd location, in the middle of a pond. The simple, whitewashed clapboard chapel stands on a little jetty that has moorings for a boat or two. The island that the chapel is named for barely breaks the surface of the water nearby and is simply a craggy pile of rock bearing a cross.

USA STATE STATS

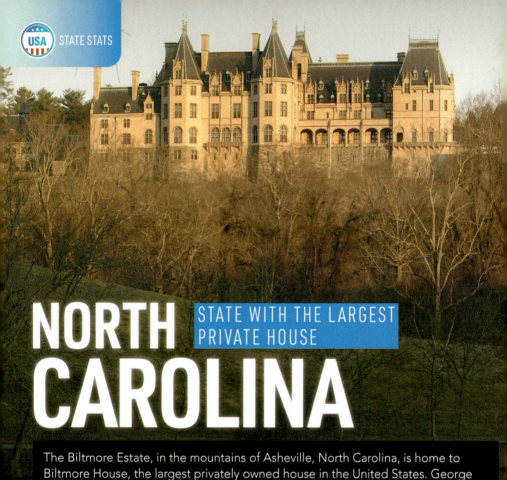

NORTH CAROLINA

STATE WITH THE LARGEST PRIVATE HOUSE

The Biltmore Estate, in the mountains of Asheville, North Carolina, is home to Biltmore House, the largest privately owned house in the United States. George Vanderbilt commissioned the 250-room French Renaissance–style chateau in 1889 and opened it to his friends and family as a country retreat in 1895. Designed by architect Richard Morris Hunt, Biltmore House has an impressive thirty-five bedrooms and forty-three bathrooms, and boasts a floor space of over 4 acres. In 1930, the Vanderbilt family opened Biltmore House to the public.

LARGEST PRIVATE HOUSES IN THE UNITED STATES
Area in square feet

- 66,400 Rennert Mansion, Sagaponack, NY
- 72,215 Pensmore, Highlandville, MO
- 84,626 Sydell Miller Mansion, Palm Beach, FL
- 109,000 Oheka Castle, Huntington, NY
- 175,000 Biltmore House, Asheville, NC

BIGGEST HONEY PRODUCER

NORTH DAKOTA

In the production of honey, North Dakota outstrips all other US states year after year. According to the USDA's National Agricultural Statistics Service, the state's 520,000 honey-producing colonies each yield an average 60 pounds of the sweet stuff per year. It seems the North Dakota climate is just right for honeybees and—more importantly—for the flowers from which they collect their nectar. Typical summer weather features warm days but cool nights.

USA STATE STATS

OHIO
FIRST LAWS PROTECTING WORKING WOMEN

In the 1800s, working conditions in US factories were grueling and pay was very low. Most of the workers were women, and it was not uncommon for them to work for twelve to fourteen hours a day, six days a week. The factories were not heated or air-conditioned, and there was no compensation for being sick. By the 1850s, several organizations had formed to improve the working conditions for women and to shorten their workday. In 1852, Ohio passed a law limiting the working day to ten hours for women under the age of eighteen. It was a small step, but it was also the first act of legislation of its kind in the United States.

ONLY US STATE CAPITOL WITH AN OIL WELL BENEATH IT

OKLAHOMA

The Oklahoma State Capitol has one very unique feature: an oil well! Affectionately named "Petunia #1" because it was built by drilling at an angle through a flower bed, it was a working well from 1942 to 1986, producing more than 1.5 million barrels of oil by the time it dried up. The bottom of the well sits about 1.25 miles under the Capitol building, and visitors can see it as part of the Capitol tour. Petunia #1 was once one of more than twenty similar wells on Capitol grounds, which are situated on the Oklahoma City Oil Field, but its rig is now the only one to remain in place, preserved as a historic monument.

STATE STATS

WORLD'S LARGEST CINNAMON ROLL
OREGON

Wolferman's Bakery holds the record for the largest cinnamon roll ever made. The spiced confection measured 9 feet long and was topped with 147 pounds of cream cheese frosting. It was made to celebrate the launch of the bakery's new 5-pound cinnamon roll. Using its popular recipe, Wolferman's needed 20 pounds of eggs, 350 pounds of flour, 378 pounds of cinnamon-sugar filling, and no fewer than 220 cinnamon sticks in their scaled-up version. The 1,150-pound cinnamon roll was transported to Medford's Annual Pear Blossom Festival in south Oregon, where visitors snapped it up for $2 a slice.

STATE THAT MANUFACTURES
THE MOST CRAYONS

PENNSYLVANIA

Easton, Pennsylvania, is home to the Crayola crayon factory and has been the company's headquarters since 1976. The factory produces an amazing twelve million crayons every single day, made from uncolored paraffin and pigment powder. In 1996, the company opened the Crayola Experience in downtown Easton. The Experience includes a live interactive show during which guests can watch a "crayonologist" make crayons, just as they are made at the factory nearby.

USA STATE STATS

STATE WITH THE OLDEST FOURTH OF JULY CELEBRATION

RHODE ISLAND

Bristol, Rhode Island, holds America's longest continuously running Fourth of July celebration. The idea for the celebration came from Revolutionary War veteran Rev. Henry Wight, of Bristol's First Congregational Church, who organized "Patriotic Exercises" to honor the nation's founders and those who fought to establish the United States. Today, Bristol begins celebrating the holiday on June 14, and puts on an array of events leading up to the Fourth itself—including free concerts, a baseball game, a Fourth of July Ball, and a half marathon.

STATE WITH THE HOTTEST PEPPER

SOUTH CAROLINA

WORLD'S HOTTEST PEPPERS
By peak heat in millions of SHU

3.18	Pepper X
2.4	Dragon's Breath
2.2	Carolina Reaper®
2	Trinidad Moruga Scorpion

Pepper X, created by Smokin' Ed Currie of Rock Hill, South Carolina, is the hottest pepper in the world, measuring an average of 3.18 million Scoville heat units (SHU). To get a feel for how hot that is, just know that a regular jalapeño clocks in at 2,500–8,000 SHU. Currie also created the world's third-hottest chili, the Carolina Reaper®. The Reaper held the record from 2013 to 2017, before being beaten by the 2.4 million SHU Dragon's Breath pepper in May. Just four months after that, Currie's Pepper X took the chili pepper world by storm.

USA STATE STATS

STATE WITH THE LARGEST SCULPTURE

SOUTH DAKOTA

While South Dakota is famous as the home of Mount Rushmore, it is also the location of another giant mountain carving: the Crazy Horse Memorial. The mountain carving, which is still in progress, will be the largest sculpture in the world when it is completed, at 563 feet tall and 641 feet long. Korczak Ziolkowski, who worked on Mount Rushmore, began the carving in 1948 to pay tribute to Crazy Horse—the Lakota leader who defeated General Custer at the Battle of the Little Bighorn. More than seventy years later, Ziolkowski's family continues his work, relying completely on funding from visitors and donors.

STATE THAT MAKES ALL THE MOONPIES
TENNESSEE

Tennessee is the home of the MoonPie, which was conceived there in 1917 by bakery salesman Earl Mitchell, Sr., after a group of local miners asked for a filling treat "as big as the moon." Made from marshmallow, graham crackers, and chocolate, the sandwich cookies were soon being mass-produced at Tennessee's Chattanooga Bakery, and MoonPie was registered as a trademark by the bakery in 1919. MoonPies first sold at just five cents each and quickly became popular—even being named the official snack of NASCAR in the late 1990s. Today, Chattanooga Bakery makes nearly a million MoonPies every day.

STATE STATS

LARGEST URBAN BAT COLONY
TEXAS

If you want to see a sky filled with hundreds of thousands of bats, head to Austin, Texas, anytime from mid-March to November. The city's Ann W. Richards Congress Avenue Bridge is home to the world's largest urban bat colony—roughly 1.5 million bats in all. The Mexican free-tailed bats first settled here in the 1980s, and numbers have grown steadily since. They currently produce around 750,000 pups per year. These days, the bats are a tourist attraction that draws about 140,000 visitors to the city, many of them hoping to catch the moment at dusk when large numbers of bats fly out from under the bridge to look for food.

UTAH
STATE WITH THE LARGEST SALTWATER LAKE

The Great Salt Lake, which inspired the name of Utah's largest city, is the largest saltwater lake in the United States, at around 75 miles long and 35 miles wide. Sometimes called "America's Dead Sea," it is typically larger than each of the states of Delaware and Rhode Island. Its size, however, fluctuates as water levels rise and fall. Since 1849, the water level has varied by as much as 20 feet, which can shift the shoreline by up to 15 miles. Great Salt Lake is too salty to support most aquatic life but is home to several kinds of algae, as well as the brine shrimp that feed on them.

USA STATE STATS

STATE THAT PRODUCES THE MOST MAPLE SYRUP
VERMONT

The state of Vermont produced 2.5 million gallons of maple syrup in 2022. The state's highest crop ever, it represents more than 50 percent of the country's total. Vermont's 1,500 maple syrup producers take sap from six million tree taps. They have to collect 40 gallons of maple sap in order to produce just 1 gallon of syrup. Producers also use maple sap for making other treats, such as maple butter, sugar, and candies.

FIRST STATE WITH WOMAN-RUN BANK
VIRGINIA

In 1903, Maggie Lena Walker opened the St. Luke Penny Savings Bank in Richmond, making Virginia the first state with a bank founded and run by a woman. A leading civil activist, Walker was also Black, making her achievement all the more remarkable in a time when the Jim Crow laws did much to restrict the advancement of Blacks in the Southern states. Through the bank and other enterprises that included a newspaper and a department store, Walker sought to provide members of the Black community with opportunities to improve their lives through employment, investment, and supporting one another's businesses.

USA STATE STATS

STATE WITH THE OLDEST GAS STATION
WASHINGTON

The Teapot Dome Service Station in Zillah, Washington, was once the oldest working gas station in the United States, and is still the only one built to commemorate a political scandal. Now preserved as a museum, the gas station was built in 1922 as a monument to the Teapot Dome Scandal, in which Albert Fall, President Warren G. Harding's secretary of the interior, took bribes to lease government oil reserves to private companies. The gas station, located on Washington's Old Highway 12, was moved in 1978 to make way for Interstate 82, then again in 2007 when the city of Zillah purchased it as a historic landmark.

STATE WITH THE LONGEST STEEL ARCH BRIDGE
WEST VIRGINIA

The New River Gorge Bridge in Fayetteville spans 3,030 feet and is 876 feet above the New River. It is both the longest and largest steel arch bridge in the United States. Builders used 88 million pounds of steel and concrete to construct it. The $37 million structure took three years to complete and opened on October 22, 1977. Bridge Day, held every October since 1980, is a BASE-jumping event at the New River Gorge Bridge. Hundreds of BASE jumpers and about 80,000 spectators gather for the one-day festival. Among the most popular events is the Big Way, in which large groups of people jump off the bridge together. During Bridge Day 2013, Donald Cripps became one of the world's oldest BASE jumpers, at eighty-four years old.

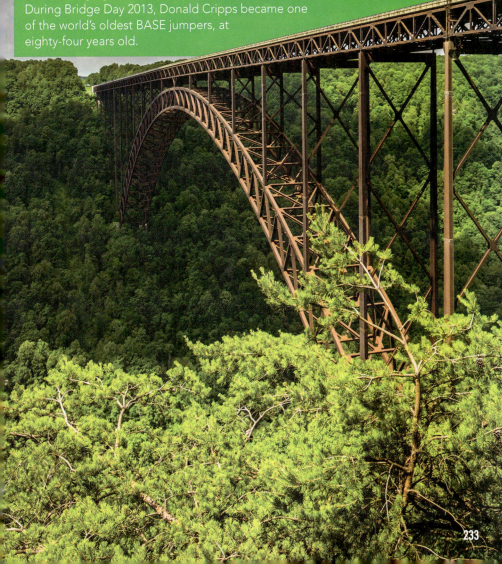

USA STATE STATS

LARGEST CROSS-COUNTRY SKI RACE

WISCONSIN

Each year in February, Wisconsin hosts America's largest cross-country ski race. The race attracts over 10,000 skiers, all attempting to complete the 55-kilometer (34-mile) course from Cable to Hayward. Milestones along the way include Boedecker Hill, Mosquito Brook, and Hatchery Park. The event is part of the Worldloppet circuit of twenty ski marathons across the globe. The winner of the 2022 race, twenty-four-year-old Leo Hipp from Minneapolis, Minnesota, completed the course in two hours, fifty-one minutes, and fifty-seven seconds.

STATE WITH THE LARGEST HOT SPRING
WYOMING

Grand Prismatic Spring, in Yellowstone National Park in Wyoming, is the largest hot spring in the United States. The spring measures 370 feet in diameter and is more than 121 feet deep; Yellowstone National Park says that the spring is bigger than a football field and deeper than a ten-story building. Grand Prismatic is not just the largest spring but also the most photographed thermal feature in Yellowstone due to its bright colors. The colors come from different kinds of bacteria, living in each part of the spring, that thrive at various temperatures. As water comes up from the middle of the spring, it is too hot to support most bacterial life, but as the water spreads out to the edges of the spring, it cools in concentric circles.

CHAPTER 9
SPORTS STARS

SPORTS STARS
TRENDING

WRESTLING SUCCESS
MOST-FOLLOWED SPORTSWOMAN ON INSTAGRAM

American judo champ Ronda Rousey is currently the world's most-followed female sports star on Instagram, with a staggering 16.5 million followers, as of February 2023. Ronda Rousey gained fame when she became the first American woman to win an Olympic judo medal (bronze) at the 2008 Games. She went on to become a star of the UFC, achieving a then-record six title defenses before signing with the WWE in 2018.

MESSI'S MOMENT OF GLORY
INSTAGRAM'S MOST-LIKED PHOTO

With seventy-five million likes, this image of Argentina's captain, Lionel Messi, holding the World Cup trophy aloft has become the most-liked photograph in Instagram history. Taken in the aftermath of Argentina's victory over France in the 2022 FIFA World Cup final, it beats the previous record of fifty-seven million likes held by an image of an ordinary brown egg.

ADIÓS, PELÉ
DEATH OF A GLOBAL SUPERSTAR

Pelé is considered to be soccer's first global superstar. On December 29, 2022, his death at the age of eighty-two sparked widespread mourning: Stadiums and landmarks around the world were lit up in his honor, Brazil entered three days of national mourning, and a staggering 230,000 people filed past his open coffin as it lay in state. A video released shortly before his death titled "Pelé did everything your favorite player did, first" went viral, attracting over thirty-six million views on Twitter.

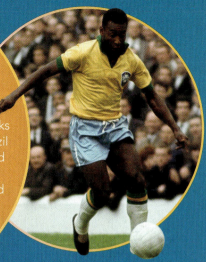

THE RISE OF THE PICKLERS
US'S FASTEST-GROWING SPORT

With an increase of 39.8 percent of participants over two years and a TikTok page attracting 374.2 million views and growing, pickleball was labeled America's fastest-growing sport in 2022. Described as a cross between tennis, Ping-Pong, and badminton, the game was created in 1965 as a backyard activity for kids. Today, it is enjoyed by an estimated 4.8 million "picklers" nationwide.

SUDDEN SCARE
HAMLIN'S HEART-STOPPING MOMENT

On January 2, 2023, during a *Monday Night Football* matchup between the Buffalo Bills and the Cincinnati Bengals, Bills' Damar Hamlin made a routine tackle of Bengals' Tee Higgins, but collapsed shortly after, having suffered a cardiac arrest. Frenzied attempts were made to resuscitate him before he was rushed to the University of Cincinnati Medical Center in critical condition. Once on the road to recovery, his first post-incident tweet was viewed 34.9 million times.

SPORTS STARS

WORLD'S LONGEST SKATEBOARD RAMP JUMP
DANNY WAY

Many extreme sports activities are showcased at the annual X Games and Winter X Games. At the 2004 X Games, held in Los Angeles, skateboarder Danny Way set an amazing record that remains unbeaten. On August 8, Way made a long-distance jump of 79 feet, beating his own 2003 world record (75 feet). In 2005, he jumped over the Great Wall of China. He made the jump despite having torn ligaments in his ankle during a practice jump on the previous day.

WORLD'S HIGHEST TIGHTROPE WALK

FREDDY NOCK

Tightrope walking looks hard enough a few feet above the ground, but Swiss stuntman Freddy Nock took it to the next level when he walked between two mountains in the Swiss Alps in March 2015. On a rope set 11,590 feet above sea level, Freddy took about thirty-nine minutes to walk the 1,140 feet across to the neighboring peak. The previous record had been held since 1974, when Frenchman Philippe Petit walked between the Twin Towers of New York's former World Trade Center.

SPORTS STARS

MAT HOFFMAN

MOST SUCCESSFUL BMX RIDER OF ALL TIME

No one has done more for the sport of BMX than Mat Hoffman. Nicknamed "The Condor," Hoffman is recognized as the greatest Vert rider in the sport, winning the World Vert Championship on ten occasions and also picking up six medals at the X Games. He is also credited with inventing more than 100 tricks, such as the 900 (which he successfully completed in 1989), a no-handed 900, a Flip faki (a backflip that includes landing backward), and a Flair (a backflip with a 180-degree turn). He also holds the world record for the highest air achieved on a BMX bike over a 24-foot quarter bike (26.5 feet) and even took his bike BASE jumping off a 3,500-foot cliff in Norway.

WORLD'S HIGHEST BASKETBALL SHOT

HOW RIDICULOUS

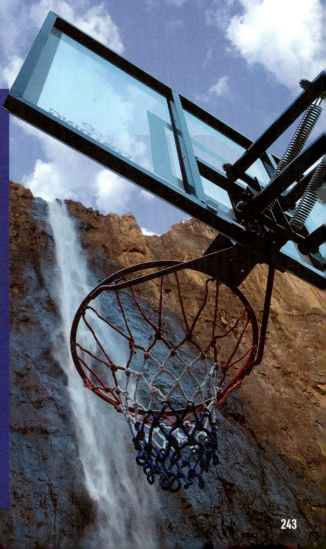

Australian trick-shot group How Ridiculous continues to break its own record. In 2015, one member made a basket from an amazing 415 feet, but the group has since improved that distance several times. In January 2018, How Ridiculous achieved its most astonishing feat yet: a basket from 660 feet, 10 inches. The group made the record shot at Maletsunyane Falls, Lesotho, in southern Africa, after five days of setup work and practice. How Ridiculous is a group of three friends who started trying trick shots for fun in their backyards in 2009. They now have a successful YouTube channel and business and are also involved in Christian charitable work.

SPORTS STARS

NBA CHAMPIONSHIP'S GREATEST RIVALRY

BOSTON CELTICS AND LA LAKERS

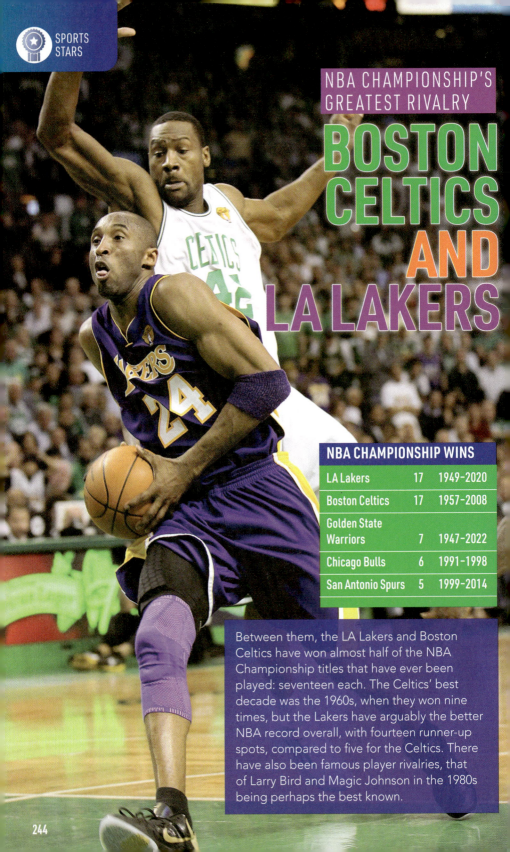

NBA CHAMPIONSHIP WINS

LA Lakers	17	1949–2020
Boston Celtics	17	1957–2008
Golden State Warriors	7	1947–2022
Chicago Bulls	6	1991–1998
San Antonio Spurs	5	1999–2014

Between them, the LA Lakers and Boston Celtics have won almost half of the NBA Championship titles that have ever been played: seventeen each. The Celtics' best decade was the 1960s, when they won nine times, but the Lakers have arguably the better NBA record overall, with fourteen runner-up spots, compared to five for the Celtics. There have also been famous player rivalries, that of Larry Bird and Magic Johnson in the 1980s being perhaps the best known.

WNBA PLAYER WITH THE MOST CAREER POINTS
DIANA TAURASI

MOST CAREER POINTS IN THE WNBA
NUMBER OF POINTS

Diana Taurasi	9,693
Tina Thompson	7,488
Tamika Catchings	7,380
Tina Charles	7,115
Candice Dupree	6,895
Cappie Pondexter	6,811

After a standout college career and three NCAA championships with the University of Connecticut Huskies, Diana Taurasi joined the Phoenix Mercury in the WNBA in 2004. Her prolific scoring helped the Mercury to its first WNBA title in 2007 (and two more since then), and her international career includes five consecutive Team USA Olympic golds, 2004–2020. Playing mainly as guard, Taurasi became the all-time leading WNBA scorer in 2017.

SPORTS STARS

YOUNGEST NBA PLAYER TO REACH 30,000 CAREER POINTS

LEBRON JAMES

On Tuesday, January 23, 2018, at age thirty-three years and twenty-four days, LeBron James became the youngest player in NBA history to reach 30,000 points, smashing Kobe Bryant's previous record. In 2020, James overtook Bryant in the career scoring list, just one day before Bryant tragically died in an aircraft accident. James has since passed 38,000 points, and in 2020 he collected the MVP award in the NBA Finals for the fourth time in his career.

NBA ACCOLADES

LeBron James was named NBA Rookie of the Year in 2004. Since that time, he has been voted the NBA's Most Valuable Player on four occasions, in 2009, 2010, 2012, and 2013.

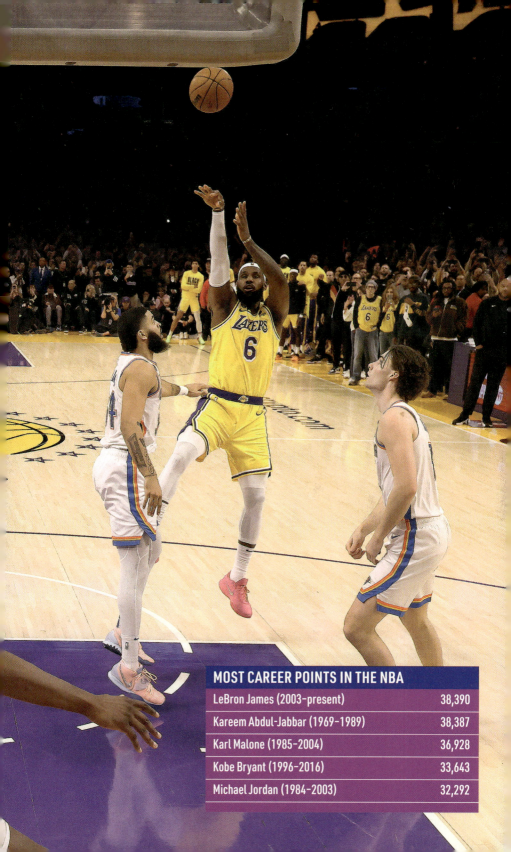

MOST CAREER POINTS IN THE NBA

LeBron James (2003–present)	38,390
Kareem Abdul-Jabbar (1969–1989)	38,387
Karl Malone (1985–2004)	36,928
Kobe Bryant (1996–2016)	33,643
Michael Jordan (1984–2003)	32,292

SPORTS STARS

JERRY RICE

NFL PLAYER WITH THE MOST CAREER TOUCHDOWNS

Jerry Rice is generally regarded as the greatest wide receiver in NFL history. He played in the NFL for twenty seasons—fifteen of them with the San Francisco 49ers—and won three Super Bowl rings. As well as leading the career touchdowns list with 208, Rice also holds the "most yards gained" mark with 23,546 yards. Most of his touchdowns were from pass receptions (197), often working with the great 49ers quarterback Joe Montana.

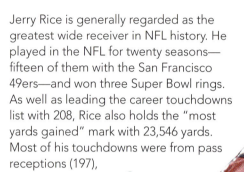

NFL PLAYERS WITH THE MOST CAREER TOUCHDOWNS
NUMBER OF TOUCHDOWNS (CAREER YEARS)

Jerry Rice	208	1985–2004
Emmitt Smith	175	1990–2004
LaDainian Tomlinson	162	2001–2011
Randy Moss	156	1998–2012
Terrell Owens	156	1996–2010

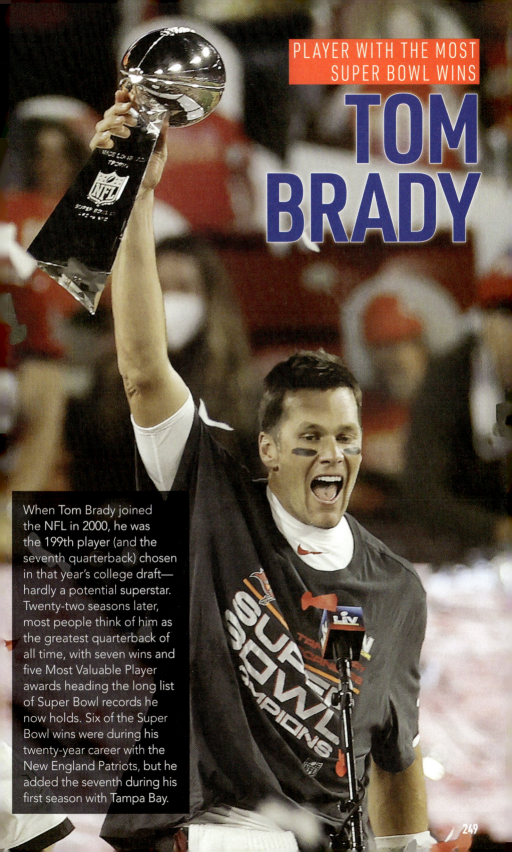

PLAYER WITH THE MOST SUPER BOWL WINS

TOM BRADY

When **Tom Brady** joined the NFL in 2000, he was the 199th player (and the seventh quarterback) chosen in that year's college draft—hardly a potential superstar. Twenty-two seasons later, most people think of him as the greatest quarterback of all time, with seven wins and five Most Valuable Player awards heading the long list of Super Bowl records he now holds. Six of the Super Bowl wins were during his twenty-year career with the New England Patriots, but he added the seventh during his first season with Tampa Bay.

SPORTS STARS

SCHOOL WITH THE MOST
ROSE BOWL WINS

USC TROJANS

The Rose Bowl is college football's oldest postseason event, first played in 1902. Taking place near January 1 of each year, the game is normally played between the Pac-12 Conference champion and the Big Ten Conference champion, but one year in three it is part of college football's playoffs. The University of Southern California has easily the best record in the Rose Bowl, with twenty-five wins from thirty-four appearances, followed by the Ohio State Buckeyes (nine wins from sixteen appearances). The Buckeyes reached that second spot on the winners' list with their 48–45 victory over the Utah Utes on New Year's Day 2022.

NEW YORK YANKEES

MLB TEAM WITH THE MOST WORLD SERIES WINS

WORLD SERIES WINS
NUMBER OF WINS

New York Yankees	27	1923-2009
St. Louis Cardinals	11	1926-2011
Oakland Athletics *	9	1910-1989
Boston Red Sox **	9	1903-2018
San Francisco Giants ***	8	1905-2014

* Previously played in Kansas City and Philadelphia
** Originally Boston Americans   *** Previously played in New York

The New York Yankees are far and away the most successful team in World Series history. Since baseball's championship was first contested in 1903, the Yankees have appeared forty times and won on twenty-seven occasions. The Yankees' greatest years were from the 1930s through the 1950s, when the team was led by legends such as Babe Ruth and Joe DiMaggio. Their nearest challengers are the St. Louis Cardinals from the National League, with eleven wins from nineteen appearances.

SPORTS STARS

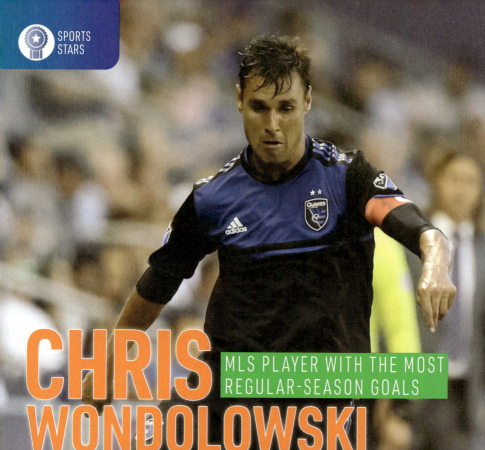

CHRIS WONDOLOWSKI

MLS PLAYER WITH THE MOST REGULAR-SEASON GOALS

MLS REGULAR-SEASON TOP SCORERS
NUMBER OF GOALS (CAREER YEARS)

Chris Wondolowski	171	2005–2021
Landon Donovan	145	2001–2016
Kei Kamara	139	2006–present
Jeff Cunningham	134	1998–2011
Jaime Moreno	133	1996–2010

Californian Chris Wondolowski took a while to get his professional soccer career going. He was drafted by the San Jose Earthquakes in a late round in 2005 but didn't earn a regular starting spot with the Quakes until 2010. Since then, however, he has scored more than ten goals for San Jose every season up to 2019. He added seven more to his total in the COVID-affected 2020 season. He scored his 171st goal in November 2021 in his final professional match. He has also earned thirty-five appearances for the US Men's National Team.

WOMAN WITH THE MOST INTERNATIONAL SOCCER CAPS

KRISTINE LILLY

WOMEN WITH THE MOST INTERNATIONAL SOCCER CAPS
NUMBER OF CAPS (CAREER YEARS)

Kristine Lilly, USA	354	1987–2010
Christine Sinclair, Canada	319	2000–present
Carli Lloyd, USA	316	2005–2021
Christie Pearce, USA	311	1997–2015
Mia Hamm, USA	276	1987–2004

In her long and successful career, Kristine Lilly played club soccer principally with the Boston Breakers. When she made her debut on the US national team in 1987, however, she was still in high school. Her total of 354 international caps is the world's highest for a man or woman, and her trophy haul includes two World Cup winner's medals and two Olympic golds.

SPORTS STARS

COUNTRY WITH THE MOST FIFA WORLD CUP WINS

BRAZIL

Brazil, host of the 2014 FIFA World Cup, has lifted the trophy the most times in the tournament's history. Germany, second on the list, has more runner-up and semifinal appearances and hence, arguably, a stronger record overall. However, many would say that Brazil's 1970 lineup, led by the incomparable Pelé, ranks as the finest team ever. The host team has won five of the twenty tournaments that have been completed to date.

FIFA WORLD CUP WINNERS
NUMBER OF WINS

Brazil	5	1958, 1962, 1970, 1994, 2002
Germany*	4	1954, 1974, 1990, 2014
Italy	4	1934, 1938, 1982, 2006
Argentina	3	1978, 1986, 2022
Uruguay	2	1930, 1950
France	2	1998, 2018

* As West Germany 1954, 1974

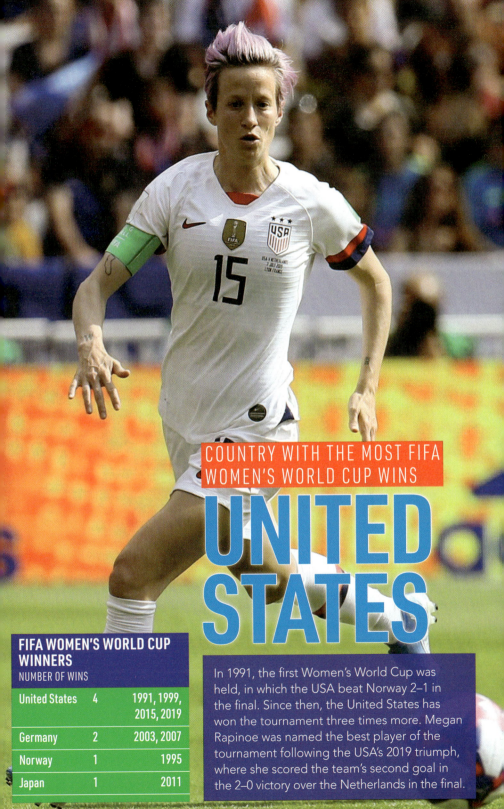

COUNTRY WITH THE MOST FIFA WOMEN'S WORLD CUP WINS

UNITED STATES

FIFA WOMEN'S WORLD CUP WINNERS
NUMBER OF WINS

United States	4	1991, 1999, 2015, 2019
Germany	2	2003, 2007
Norway	1	1995
Japan	1	2011

In 1991, the first Women's World Cup was held, in which the USA beat Norway 2–1 in the final. Since then, the United States has won the tournament three times more. Megan Rapinoe was named the best player of the tournament following the USA's 2019 triumph, where she scored the team's second goal in the 2–0 victory over the Netherlands in the final.

SPORTS STARS

MOST BALLON D'OR WINS
LIONEL MESSI

A skilled playmaker, Argentina's Lionel Messi is considered by many to be the greatest soccer player of his generation. Before moving to French team Paris Saint-Germain in 2021, Messi had spent almost his entire career with Barcelona, his team winning thirty-five trophies. He holds the all-time record for the most La Liga goals (474) and the most international goals by a South American player (ninety-eight). He is also the only player in the game's history to have won the Ballon d'Or, awarded annually since 1956 to the world's best player, on seven occasions (in 2009, 2010, 2011, 2012, 2015, 2019, and 2021).

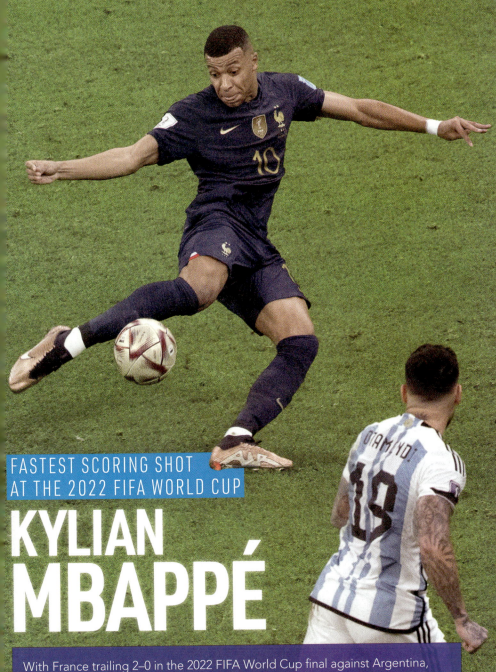

FASTEST SCORING SHOT AT THE 2022 FIFA WORLD CUP

KYLIAN MBAPPÉ

With France trailing 2–0 in the 2022 FIFA World Cup final against Argentina, their star player Kylian Mbappé managed to drag his team back into the game. First, in the eightieth minute, he converted a penalty; ninety-seven seconds later, he made a stunning strike from the edge of the penalty area—clocked at 76.67 mph, it was the fastest scoring shot recorded at the tournament. The star scored from the spot again in extra time to become only the second player in history to net a hat-trick in a FIFA World Cup final (after England's Geoff Hurst in 1966). But his World Cup final dream ended in disappointment; Argentina went on to win the penalty shootout 4–2 to lift the trophy for the third time.

SPORTS STARS

WOMAN WITH THE MOST GRAND SLAMS IN OPEN ERA

SERENA WILLIAMS

Serena Williams is truly one of the all-time greats in tennis, playing with a combination of power and athleticism that has made her almost unbeatable when she's been at her best. Williams first won a Grand Slam singles title at the US Open in 1999 and has since added five more, plus three in France and seven each in Australia and at Wimbledon. She's tough to beat in doubles, too. She and her sister Venus Williams have reached fourteen Grand Slam finals together—and won them all.

SERENA WILLIAMS GRAND SLAMS
FINALS WINS

US Open	1999, 2002, 2008, 2012, 2013, 2014
Australian Open	2003, 2005, 2007, 2009, 2010, 2015, 2017
French Open	2002, 2013, 2015
Wimbledon	2002, 2003, 2009, 2010, 2012, 2015, 2016

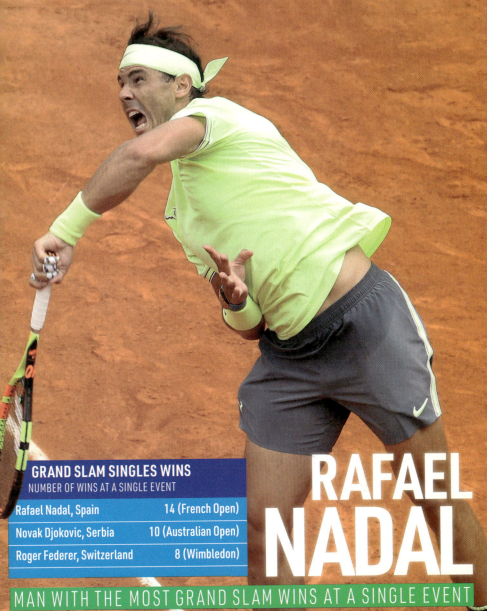

RAFAEL NADAL

GRAND SLAM SINGLES WINS
NUMBER OF WINS AT A SINGLE EVENT

Rafael Nadal, Spain	14 (French Open)
Novak Djokovic, Serbia	10 (Australian Open)
Roger Federer, Switzerland	8 (Wimbledon)

MAN WITH THE MOST GRAND SLAM WINS AT A SINGLE EVENT

History has yet to determine who will end up becoming the most successful male tennis player in history, with Spain's Rafael Nadal and Serbia's Novak Djokovic vying for the crown for the most Grand Slam wins. But there is no doubt that the Spaniard's feats on the clay of Roland-Garros will be remembered by tennis fans forever. From the moment Nadal first claimed the French Open title in 2005, he has become almost unbeatable on the surface—and has rightly earned the moniker the "King of Clay." By 2022, Nadal had played in a total of 115 matches at the venue, with only three defeats (winning 333 of the 367 sets he has contested), and he has claimed a staggering 14 French Open titles.

SPORTS STARS

NHL TEAM WITH THE MOST STANLEY CUP WINS

MONTREAL CANADIENS

The Montreal Canadiens are the oldest and, by far, the most successful National Hockey League team. In its earliest years, the Stanley Cup had various formats, but since 1927, it has been awarded exclusively to the champion NHL team—and the Canadiens have won it roughly one year in every four. Their most successful years were the 1940s through the 1970s, when the team was inspired by all-time greats like Maurice Richard and Guy Lafleur.

STANLEY CUP WINNERS (SINCE 1915)
NUMBER OF WINS (TIME SPAN)

Montreal Canadiens	24	1916-1993
Toronto Maple Leafs	13	1918-1967
Detroit Red Wings	11	1936-2008
Boston Bruins	6	1929-2011
Chicago Blackhawks	6	1934-2015

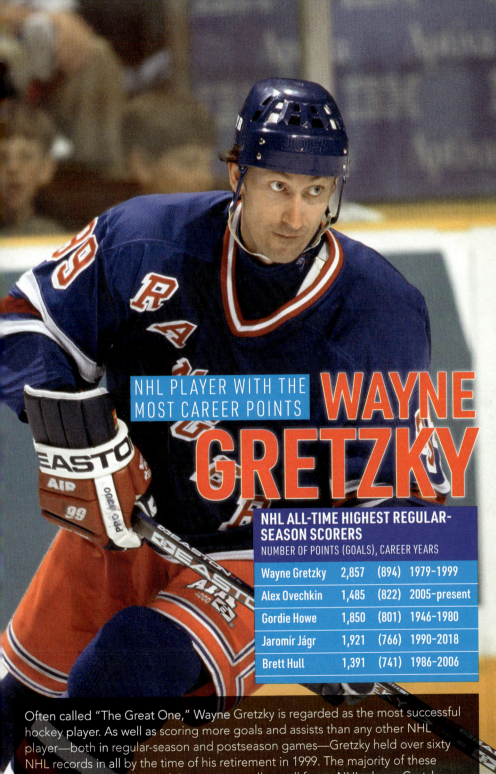

NHL PLAYER WITH THE MOST CAREER POINTS
WAYNE GRETZKY

NHL ALL-TIME HIGHEST REGULAR-SEASON SCORERS
NUMBER OF POINTS (GOALS), CAREER YEARS

Wayne Gretzky	2,857	(894)	1979–1999
Alex Ovechkin	1,485	(822)	2005–present
Gordie Howe	1,850	(801)	1946–1980
Jaromír Jágr	1,921	(766)	1990–2018
Brett Hull	1,391	(741)	1986–2006

Often called "The Great One," Wayne Gretzky is regarded as the most successful hockey player. As well as scoring more goals and assists than any other NHL player—both in regular-season and postseason games—Gretzky held over sixty NHL records in all by the time of his retirement in 1999. The majority of these records still stand. Although he was unusually small for an NHL player, Gretzky had great skills and an uncanny ability to be in the right place at the right time.

SPORTS STARS

MANON RHÉAUME

FIRST WOMAN TO PLAY IN AN NHL GAME

Manon Rhéaume had a fine career as a goaltender in women's ice hockey, earning World Championship gold medals with the Canadian National Women's Team. She is also the first—and only—woman to play for an NHL club. On September 23, 1992, she played one period for the Tampa Bay Lightning in an exhibition game against the St. Louis Blues, during which she saved seven of nine shots. She later played twenty-four games for various men's teams in the professional International Hockey League.

MOST CONSECUTIVE NASCAR CHAMPIONSHIP WINS

JIMMIE JOHNSON

The NASCAR drivers' championship has been contested since 1949. California native Jimmie Johnson is tied at the top of the all-time wins list with seven, but his five-season streak, 2006–2010, is easily the best in the sport's history. Johnson's racing career began on 50cc motorcycles when he was five years old. All of his NASCAR championship wins were achieved driving Chevrolets. He won eighty-three NASCAR races in his career, the last in 2017. He retired from NASCAR in 2020 but still competes in IndyCar events.

NASCAR CHAMPIONSHIP WINS
NUMBER OF WINS (YEARS IN WHICH THE TITLE WAS WON)

Jimmie Johnson	7	2006, 2007, 2008, 2009, 2010, 2013, 2016
Dale Earnhardt, Sr.	7	1980, 1986, 1987, 1990, 1991, 1993, 1994
Richard Petty	7	1964, 1967, 1971, 1972, 1974, 1975, 1979
Jeff Gordon	4	1995, 1997, 1998, 2001

SPORTS STARS

ALL-TIME MOST SUCCESSFUL FEMALE SNOWBOARD CROSS COMPETITOR

LINDSEY JACOBELLIS

Snowboard cross races were only invented in the 1990s, and for much of their history since then, Lindsey Jacobellis has been the dominant female athlete in the event. Coming up to the 2022 Winter Olympics, Jacobellis had won six World Championships and taken gold ten times at the Winter X Games, but her best Olympic performance, in four attempts, had been a silver in 2006, when she blew a winning lead by celebrating before she crossed the finish line. She finally got it right in Beijing, though, taking two golds for Team USA, in the individual event and the mixed team.

JACOBELLIS'S MEDAL TALLY

Olympics	2 golds, 1 silver
World Championships	6 golds, 1 bronze
Winter X Games	10 golds, 1 silver, 1 bronze

Erin Jackson gained her first big sporting successes as an in-line speed skater and in roller derby. Jackson was an in-line-skating medalist in the 2015 Pan-American Games, and it was only in 2016 that she switched to speed skating on ice. She lacked experience at her first Olympics in 2018 but did everything right in Beijing in 2022. Her winning time of 37.04 seconds in the 500-meter race gave her a 0.08-second margin of victory. There are two types of indoor ice-skating races. Long-track races in international competitions take place on a 400-meter circuit, similar in size to a standard running track. Short-track races take place on a circuit created on an international-size hockey rink. The long-track races are faster, but the short-track ones can be very dramatic, with many crashes and falls.

FIRST BLACK WOMAN TO WIN AN INDIVIDUAL WINTER OLYMPIC GOLD MEDAL

ERIN JACKSON

SPORTS STARS

Nathan Chen made skating history at the 2018 Winter Olympics by being the first-ever skater to attempt and land six quadruple jumps during one performance. Quad jumps—in which the skater spins around four times while in the air—are among the hardest moves in skating, and grouping several of them in one program makes them more difficult still. Chen's record-breaking moves did not win a medal, because he skated poorly in another part of the competition, but he won the 2018 World Championship after landing his six quads once again. He retained his title in 2019 and added a third world gold in 2021. Chen finally won Olympic gold at Beijing in 2022 in the men's singles competition, though this time attempting "only" five quad jumps in his free skate program.

FIRST-EVER SKATER TO LAND SIX QUADRUPLE JUMPS

NATHAN CHEN

MOST WINTER OLYMPICS SNOWBOARDING GOLD MEDALS
SHAUN WHITE

A professional skateboarder, successful musician, and Olympic and X Games star, Shaun White has an astonishing range of talents. He has won more X Games gold medals than anyone else, but his three Olympic golds, in the halfpipe competitions in 2006, 2010, and 2018, the most ever by a snowboarder, are perhaps his biggest achievement. The best of all was in 2018, when he landed two super-difficult back-to-back tricks in the final round to jump into first place. White's medal happened to be the USA's 100th at the Winter Olympics. White again made the USA Olympic team for Beijing 2022, just missing out on another medal with fourth place in the halfpipe. He announced his retirement from competition after this event.

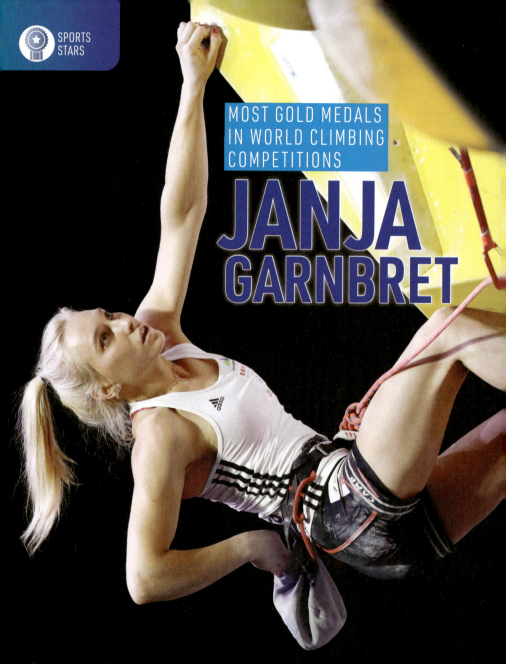

SPORTS STARS

MOST GOLD MEDALS IN WORLD CLIMBING COMPETITIONS

JANJA GARNBRET

Competition climbing has recently become an Olympic sport. Climbers compete on indoor climbing walls in three disciplines—lead climbing, speed climbing, and bouldering—to arrive at a combined score for a medal. Janja Garnbret, who is from Slovenia, has won more gold medals than any other climber, male or female, in World Championships and World Cup events. She has won the combined event World Cup series every year since 2016, and over the same period won six golds at the World Championships, including two individual golds and the combined gold medal in 2019. In 2021, Garnbret won the first-ever women's Olympic gold medal awarded in her sport; the winner of the men's competition in Tokyo was Alberto Ginés of Spain.

HIGHEST POLE VAULT

ARMAND DUPLANTIS

Born in 1999 and raised in Louisiana by an American father and Swedish mother, Armand "Mondo" Duplantis started setting pole-vault records when he was still in elementary school. After choosing to compete for his mother's homeland, he landed his first big win in adult competition in the 2018 European Championships. In 2019, he gained a silver medal in the World Championships, but in 2022 he moved ahead of the field in his event, setting a new world record of 6.21 meters (20 feet, 4.25 inches). These records were in indoor competitions, but in 2020 Duplantis also achieved the best-ever outdoor jump—6.15 meters—though this is not an official world record.

SPORTS STARS

MOST SUCCESSFUL SURFER OF ALL TIME
KELLY SLATER

Born on February 11, 1972, Kelly Slater grew up in Cocoa Beach, Florida, and started surfing at the age of five. By age ten, he was winning age-division events up and down the Atlantic coast and, in 1984, he won his first age-division national title. He turned professional in 1990, won his first pro event—the Rip Curl Pro in France—in 1992, and ended the year by becoming world champion for the first time. He claimed five successive world titles between 1994 and 1998 before taking a break from the sport—only to return in 2002 and earn a further five titles between 2005 and 2011. His haul of eleven World Surf League titles is an all-time record.

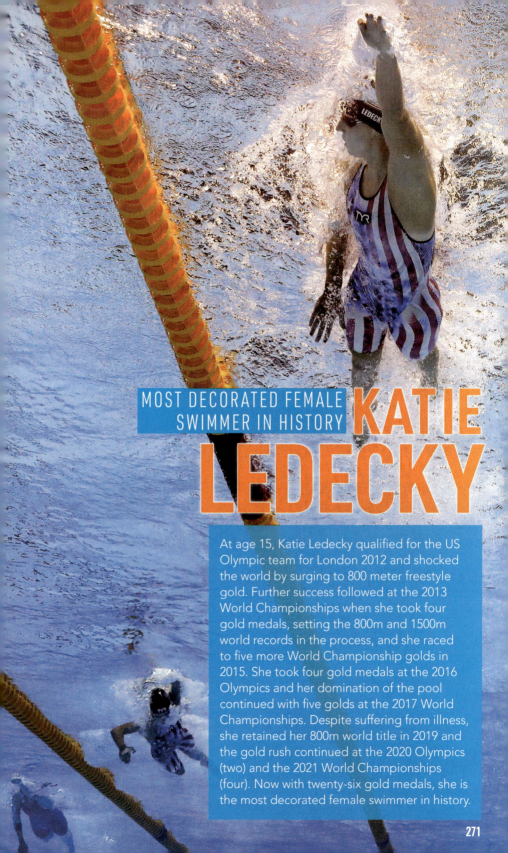

KATIE LEDECKY

MOST DECORATED FEMALE SWIMMER IN HISTORY

At age 15, Katie Ledecky qualified for the US Olympic team for London 2012 and shocked the world by surging to 800 meter freestyle gold. Further success followed at the 2013 World Championships when she took four gold medals, setting the 800m and 1500m world records in the process, and she raced to five more World Championship golds in 2015. She took four gold medals at the 2016 Olympics and her domination of the pool continued with five golds at the 2017 World Championships. Despite suffering from illness, she retained her 800m world title in 2019 and the gold rush continued at the 2020 Olympics (two) and the 2021 World Championships (four). Now with twenty-six gold medals, she is the most decorated female swimmer in history.

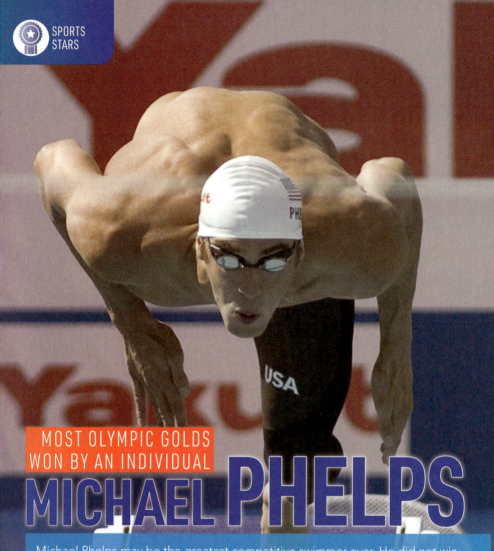

SPORTS STARS

MOST OLYMPIC GOLDS WON BY AN INDIVIDUAL
MICHAEL PHELPS

Michael Phelps may be the greatest competitive swimmer ever. He did not win any medals at his first Olympics in 2000, but at each of the Summer Games from 2004 through 2016, he was the most successful individual athlete of any nation. When he announced his retirement after London 2012, he was already the most decorated Olympic athlete ever—but he didn't stay retired for long. At Rio 2016, he won five more golds and a silver, taking his medal total to twenty-eight—twenty-three of them gold.

MOST SUCCESSFUL OLYMPIANS
NUMBER OF MEDALS WON (GOLD)

Michael Phelps, USA	Swimming	2004–2016	28 (23)
Larisa Latynina, USSR	Gymnastics	1956–1964	18 (9)
Marit Bjørgen, Norway	Cross-country skiing	2002–2018	15 (8)
Nikolai Andrianov, USSR	Gymnastics	1972–1980	15 (7)

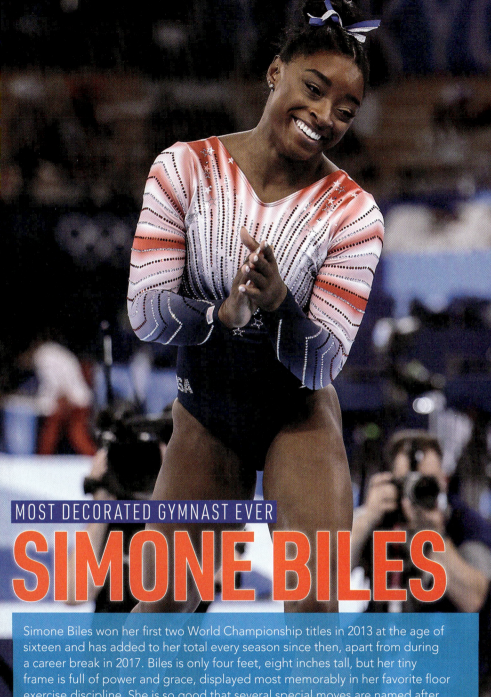

MOST DECORATED GYMNAST EVER
SIMONE BILES

Simone Biles won her first two World Championship titles in 2013 at the age of sixteen and has added to her total every season since then, apart from during a career break in 2017. Biles is only four feet, eight inches tall, but her tiny frame is full of power and grace, displayed most memorably in her favorite floor exercise discipline. She is so good that several special moves are named after her—and they are so difficult that she is the only competitor so far to perform these in championships. To date, she has won four Olympic and nineteen World Championship gold medals. Biles has also been widely praised as a champion for mental health awareness and for her bravery in speaking out as a victim in an abuse scandal in her sport.

SPORTS STARS

SYDNEY MCLAUGHLIN

WORLD RECORD HOLDER IN WOMEN'S 400-METER HURDLES

New Jersey native Sydney McLaughlin triumphed at the 2021 Tokyo Olympics in perhaps the greatest track race of the Games. McLaughlin had set a new world record of 51.90 seconds in the US Olympic trials, edging ahead of her great rival Dalilah Muhammad. Muhammad smashed that mark with 51.58 in the Tokyo final, but McLaughlin stayed in front with an astonishing 51.46 win. She went on to better that mark, clocking a staggering 50.68 seconds in Eugene, Oregon, on July 22, 2022.

FASTEST WOMEN'S 400M HURDLES

Sydney McLaughlin (USA)	50.68	2022
Sydney McLaughlin (USA)	51.41	2022
Sydney McLaughlin (USA)	51.46	2021
Dalilah Muhammad (USA)	51.58	2021
Sydney McLaughlin (USA)	51.61	2022

FASTEST MAN IN THE WORLD
USAIN BOLT

Jamaica's top athlete, Usain Bolt, is the greatest track sprinter who has ever lived. Other brilliant Olympic finalists have described how all they can do is watch as Bolt almost disappears into the distance. Usain's greatest victories have been his triple Olympic gold medals at London 2012 and Rio 2016, plus two gold medals from Beijing 2008. Usain also holds the 100-meter world record (9.58s) and the 200-meter record (19.19s), both from the 2009 World Championships.

FASTEST 100M SPRINTS OF ALL TIME
TIME IN SECONDS

Usain Bolt (Jamaica)	9.58	Berlin 2009
Usain Bolt (Jamaica)	9.63	London 2012
Usain Bolt (Jamaica)	9.69	Beijing 2008
Tyson Gay (USA)	9.69	Shanghai 2009
Yohan Blake (Jamaica)	9.69	Lausanne 2012

SPORTS STARS

MOST DECORATED PARALYMPIAN EVER
TRISCHA ZORN

Trischa Zorn is the most successful Paralympian of all time, having won an astonishing fifty-five medals, forty-one of them gold, at the Paralympic Games from 1980 to 2004. She won every Paralympic event she entered from 1980 to 1988. Zorn is blind and helps military veterans with disabilities enter the world of parasport. Zorn was inducted into the Paralympic Hall of Fame in 2012.

LEADING PARALYMPIC MEDALISTS
NUMBER OF MEDALS WON

Trischa Zorn, USA	55
Heinz Frei, Switzerland	35
Jonas Jacobsson, Sweden	30
Zipora Rubin-Rosenbaum, Israel	30
Jessica Long, USA	29

COUNTRY WITH THE MOST ALL-TIME PARALYMPIC MEDALS
USA

Although China topped the Paralympic medal table at the 2022 Winter Games in Beijing (61 medals), with the United States coming in fifth (20 medals), the United States comfortably leads the all-time medal count in the Paralympic Summer Games. Norway heads the standings in the Winter Games, with the United States in third place, giving the United States an overall medal total that will be unbeatable for many years to come.

COUNTRIES WITH THE MOST PARALYMPIC MEDALS
TOTAL NUMBER OF MEDALS WON

United States	2,618
Great Britain	1,954
Germany*	1,934
China	1,299
France	1,275

* includes totals of former East and West Germany

INDEX

A
Abdul-Jabbar, Kareem 247
Abu Dhabi 60
Abyssinian 154
Activision Blizzard 101
Actor 27, 29, 35, 38, 39
Actress 24, 25, 27, 31, 33, 34, 35, 38, 45
African bush elephant 116
Air Max sneakers 87
Aircraft 49, 56
Alabama 186
Alaska 113, 187
Albertsons Stadium 197
Album, music 8, 9, 11, 12, 14, 16, 18, 19, 20, 21
Aleut 187
Algae 229
Alligator 194
Alps 48
Amazon River 172
American Music Awards 13, 21
Amphitheater 190
Amur tiger 121
Amusement park 61
Andrianov, Nikolai 272
Angora rabbit 148
Ann W. Richards Congress Avenue Bridge 228
Annie 34
Anoka 208
Ant 142
Antarctica 139, 166
Antiracism protest 93
Antler 113, 191
Apollo 10 58-59
Apps 90
Arabian Desert 170
Arachnophobia 140
Arch-gravity dam 188
Argentina 149, 238, 254, 256, 257
Arizona 188
Arkansas 189
Arm span 118
Art gallery 64
"As It Was" 8
Asian elephant 116
Asian giant hornet 141
"The Astronaut" 13
AstroTurf 197
Auction 98
Australia 65, 114, 125, 132, 169, 170
Australian Open 258
Avatar: The Way of Water 40
Avengers: Endgame 32
Avengers: Infinity War 32
Avian flu 146
Axiom Space 49
Azerbaijan 171

B
"Baby Shark Dance" 91
Bad Bunny 8, 20
"Bad Decisions" 13
"Bad to the Bone" school bus 50
Bailey, Halle 25
Bald eagle 136
Ballet 209
Ballon d'Or 256
Bank 231
Barbie 38
BASE jumping 233, 242
Baseball 195, 199, 251
Basketball 243, 244-247
Bat 117, 228
Batagaika Crater 176
"Bath Song" 37
Battle of the Little Bighorn 226
Beagle 69, 151
Bear 113
Beasts of the Southern Wild 34
Beatles, The 14, 190
Beaver Stadium 67
Bee 141, 219
Beluga sturgeon 171
"Best I Ever Had" 12
Beyoncé 19
Bialik, Mayim 28
Bieber, Justin 8
Big cat 121
Big Toyz Racing 52
Biles, Simone 273
Billboard 87
Billboard charts 6, 12, 14, 20
Billboard Music Awards 13
Billy Elliot: The Musical 44
Biltmore House 218
Biodiversity 159
Bird 120, 134-140, 146
Bison 201
Bjørgen, Marit 272
Black Panther 32, 40
Black Panther: Wakanda Forever 40
Black Rock Desert 54
Blake, Yohan 275
Blanco, Benny 13
Bleymaier, Gene 197
Blokhus Sculpture Park 81
Bloodhound 54
Blue whale 127
BMX 242
Bogotá 76
Bolivia 69
Bolt, Usain 275
Borneo 132
Boston Breakers 253
Boston Bruins 260
Boston Celtics 244
Boston Red Sox 251
Botswana 120
Box office 29, 32, 40-41

C
Brady, Tom 249
Brazil 177, 254
"Break My Soul" 19
Bridge 74, 181, 228, 233
Brine shrimp 229
Bristlecone pine 160
Bristol, Rhode Island 224
British shorthair 154
British Sign Language 7
Broadway show 42-44
Brooks, Garth 14
Brown, Barnum 211
Brown, Millie Bobby 25, 31, 38
Bryant, Kobe 246, 247
BTS 7, 13
Buffalo Bills 239
Bugatti 51
Bull shark 129
Bulldog 151
Bullock, Sandra 38
Burj Khalifa 70-71
Busan Asiad Main Stadium 7
Bush, Kate 6

California 75, 158, 160, 161, 174, 179, 190
Californian redwood 161
Call of Duty 101, 103
Cambridge Medical Robotics 107
Camel 112
Cameron, James 40
Campbell, Brad and Jen 52
Candy 192
Candy Crush Saga 90
Cape Canaveral 58
Capitol building 65, 205, 221
Car 49, 51, 54
Career points 245, 247, 261
Carell, Steve 29
Carey, Mariah 17
Carlin Trend 213
Carolina Reaper 225
Caspian Sea 171
Castle 80
Cat 97, 146, 154-155
Catchings, Tamika 245
Cathedral 80
Cats 42
Cave 164-165
Caviar 171
Cedar Creek Fire 174
Centipede 142
Challengers 38
Chameleon 133
Change.org petition 93
Charles, James 94
Charles, Tina 245
Charlie Brown lunar module 58
Chattanooga Bakery 227
Chauvin, Derek 93

278

Cheetah 120
Chef Pii 185
Chen, Nathan 266
Chernow, Ron 44
Chicago 42
Chicago Blackhawks 260
Chicago Bulls 244
Chicken Shop Date 25
Chicken wing 25
Chihuahua 153
Chile 73, 167
China 55, 66, 72, 74, 78–79, 86, 168, 172, 240, 277
Chomolungma 168
Chu, Dr. Betty 148
Church 217
Cincinnati Bengals 30, 239
Cincinnati Red Stockings 199
Cincinnati Zoo 120
Cinnamon roll 222
Citystars 73
Civil rights activist 231
Clam garden 185
Climate change 159, 176
Climbing 268
Coast Douglas-fir 161
Coastal Carolina Chanticleers 197
CoComelon Nursery Rhymes 37
Coldplay 13
Colman, Olivia 27
Colombia 76
Colorado 179, 191
Colorado River 188
Colosseum 65
Colugo 115
Connecticut 192
Connor, Kit 27
Coral reef 169
Corleone, Chencho 8
Cotton, Coby 86
Country music 17, 18, 21
Country Music Awards 18
Country Music Hall of Fame 18
COVID-19 pandemic 81, 86, 252
Crab 193
Cramps 24
Crater 176
Crater of Diamonds 189
Crawfish 203
Crayola Experience 223
Crayon 223
Crazy Horse Memorial 226
Cripps, Donald 233
Crocodile 132, 194
Cross Island Chapel 217
Cross-country skiing 234
Cruise ship 82
Cruise, Tom 38, 39, 40
Crystal Lagoons 73
"Cuff It" 19
Cunningham, Jeff 252
Currie, Smokin' Ed 225

Custer, General 226
Cutworm moth 143
Cyclone 178
Cyrus, Billy Ray 17
Czech Republic 73, 80

D

Dachshund 151
Daddy Yankee 10
Dahl, Roald 45
Dam 188
D'Amelio, Charli 95
Dance 209
Dance, Thomas 205
Danyang-Kunshan Grand Bridge 74
Dead Sea 166
Deaf Talent Collective 7
Delaware 193
Demetriou, Cleo 45
Democratic party 185
Dengue fever 144
Denman Glacier 166
Denmark 81
Desert 54, 83, 143, 170, 212
Desert Dome 212
Desert locust 143
"Despacito" 10, 17, 91
Despicable Me 29, 41
Despicable Me 2 41
Despicable Me 3 41
Detroit Red Wings 260
Devon Rex 154
Diamond 189
Diamante Cabo San Lucas 73
DiCaprio, Leonardo 39
DiMaggio, Joe 251
Dimoldenberg, Amelia 25
Diner 215
Dinosaur 127, 211
Disease 144
Disney 7, 25, 43, 184
Disney Brothers Cartoon Studio 184
Disney, Walt 184
Divide 11
Djokovic, Novak 259
Doctor Strange in the Multiverse of Madness 40
Dog 69, 96, 147, 150–151, 153
Dog Bark Park Inn 69
Donaldson, Jimmy (MrBeast) 106
Donovan, Landon 252
Doyle, Rob 48
Draco 115
Dracula ant 142
Dragonfly 145
Dragon's Breath 225
Drake 12
Dubai 49, 66, 70–71
Dude Perfect 86
Dun, Joshua 15
Duplantis, Armand 269
Dupree, Candice 245

E

Eagle 136
Eagles, The 14
Ear 116
Earnhardt, Dale, Sr. 263
Earnings 6, 13, 16, 31, 36, 38, 39, 41, 89, 106
Earthquake 158
Egg 137, 139, 145
Egypt 73, 83
El Tatio 167
El Ultimo Tour del Mundo 20
Eldorado National Forest 174
Electric car 49
Elephant 116
Elevator 70
Elizabeth II, Queen 87
Elk 191
Emancipation 39
Emmanuel 146
Emmy Awards 27
Emoji 92
Emperor penguin 138–139
Emu 146
Encanto 7
Encephalitis 144
Enchilada 216
Enola Holmes 2 31, 38
Epaulette shark 125
"Eras Tour" 7
Estrada, Roberto 216
Eucalyptus 114
Evans, Sean 25
Everest 168
Everest, Sir George 168
Everglades National Park 194
Everything Everywhere All at Once 33
Exotic shorthair 154
Eyak 187

F

Face Holding Back Tears 92
Falabella miniature horse 149
Fall, Albert 232
Fanny 108–109
Fayetteville 233
Feathers 135
Federer, Roger 259
Fenelon Place Elevator 200
Fenty Beauty 16
Fergie 112
Ferrari World 60
FIFA Women's World Cup 255
FIFA World Cup 88, 238, 254, 257
Fireworks 202
Fish 125, 128–129, 171
Fishtopher 144
Flint Hills 201
Florida 136, 194, 218
Floyd, George 93
Flying fish 115
Flying lemur 115

279

INDEX

Flying lizard 115
Flying squid 115
Flying squirrel 115
Folklore 9
Fonsi, Luis 10, 17, 91
Football 30, 239, 248-250
Football field 197
Forbes, Harper 112
Forbes top-earners list 16, 36
Forest City 199
Formula Rossa 60
Fossil 211
Fourth of July 224
France 175, 238, 254, 257, 258, 270, 277
Franchesca 148
Franchise, movie 32, 41
Franchise, videogame 103
Freestanding building 72
Frei, Heinz 276
French bulldog 151
French Open 258, 259
Frog 131
Frozen II 41

G

G-force 60
Gabeira, Maya 173
Galápagos penguin 138
Game app 90
Games console 102
Garden, vertical 76
Garnbret, Janja 268
Gas station 232
Gay, Tyson 275
General Earth Minerals 189
Gentoo penguin 138
Georgia, USA 195
German shepherd 151
German short-haired pointer 151
Germany 254, 255, 277
Gerwig, Greta 38
Geyser 167
Giant sequoia 161
Gienger, Travis 208
Ginés, Alberto 268
Giraffe 122-123
Gironde Fires 175
Glacier 166
Glass Animals 8
Global warming 159, 176
Globe skimmer 145
Gold 213
Golden Globe awards 34
Golden retriever 151
Golden State Warriors 244
Goliath bird-eating tarantula 140
"Goo Goo Muck" 24
Gordon, Jeff 263
Gorilla 118
Gosling, Ryan 38

Grammer, Kelsey 26
Grammy Awards 19
Grand Prismatic Spring 235
Grand Slam 258, 259
Grand Theft Auto 103
Graves, J.K. 200
Great Barrier Reef 125, 169
Great Britain 44, 53, 58, 277
Great Lakes 207
Great Salt Lake 229
Great Sphinx 83
Great Victoria Desert 170
Great Wall of China 240
Great white shark 129
Greater Philadelphia Expo Center 105
Green wall 76
Gregory Brothers 6
Gretzky, Wayne 261
Guinness World Records 80, 96, 97, 104, 105
Guns N' Roses 11
Gymnastics 273

H

Hailstone 180
Hale, Sarah Josepha 206
Halloween 184, 208
Hamilton 44
Hamilton, Alexander 44
Hamilton Field 199
Hamlin, Damar 239
Hamm, Mia 253
Hamwi, Ernest 210
Hang Son Doong 164-165
Harding, Warren G. 232
Harrison, Darren 49
Harry Potter 32
Harry's House 8
Hawaii 196
Hawking, Stephen 26
Heart Hands 92
Heartstopper 27
Heat dome 158
Heat wave 158, 178
"Heat Waves" 8
Hell Creek Formation 211
Henry, Justin 35
Henry Doorly Zoo 212
Hillary, Sir Edmund 168
Himalayas 168
Hip-hop 44
Hipp, Leo 234
Hoatzin 134
Hoffman, Dustin 35
Hoffman, Mat 242
Hollywood Bowl Orchestra 190
Honey 219
Hong Kong 66, 82
Honolulu 196
Hoover Dam 188

Hornet 141
Horse 149
Horsefly 143
Horseshoe crab 193
Hot Ones 25
Hot spring 235
Hotel 64, 68-69
Hotel Palacio de Sal 69
"Hotline Bling" 12
House 64, 218
House Zero 64
How Ridiculous 243
Howe, Gordie 261
Howler monkey 124
Hubble Space Telescope 77
Huddleston, John Wesley 189
Hull, Brett 261
Hunga Tonga-Hunga Ha'apai 159
Hungarian sheepdog 150
Hunt, Richard Morris 218
Hurdles 274
Hurricane Harbor Chicago 61
Hveravellir 167
Hydroelectric power 188
Hydrogen fuel cell 48
Hydropower 48
Hyoid bone 124
Hyperion 161

I

"I Want to Hold Your Hand" 14
Ice cream cone 210
Ice hockey 260-262
Ice skating 265-266
Iceland 167
ICON 64
Idaho 69, 167, 197
If You're Reading This It's Too Late 12
Illinois 198
Illusionist 94
In-line speed skating 265
India 181
Indiana 199
Indonesia 125, 130
Ingram, Kerry 45
Insect 141-145, 219
Instagram 7, 64, 88, 96-97, 238
International Ballet Competition 209
International Commerce Centre 66
International Day of Sign Languages 7
International Hockey League 262
International soccer caps 253
International Space Station 49
Inuit 187
Iolani Palace 196
Iowa 200
Iran 171
Italy 254
"It's Corn" 6

J

Jack-o'-lantern 208
Jackson, Erin 265
Jackson, Michael 21
Jacobellis, Lindsey 264
Jacobsson, Jonas 276
Jágr, Jaromir 261
Jaguar 121
Jain, Prakrit 112
Jalapeño 225
James Bond 32
James, LeBron 246-247
James Webb Space Telescope 77
Japan 87, 98, 209, 255
Jay-Z 19
Jeffries, Hakeem 185
Jennings, Ken 28
Jeopardy! 28
Jiffpom 96
John, Elton 11
Johns Hopkins University 57
Johnson, Jimmie 263
Joker 2 38
Jonathan 152
Jones, Bobby 195
Jordan 166
Jordan, Michael 247
Jordan Rift Valley 166
Judo 238
Jurassic World: Dominion 40

K

K-pop 7, 13
K2 168
Kagera River 172
Kaji, Ryan 36
Kalahari Desert 170
Kalakaua, King 196
Kamara, Kel 252
Kanchenjunga 168
Kansas 201
Kardashian, Kim 24
Kazakhstan 171
Kekiongas 199
Kennedy, John F. 24
Kennedy Space Center 49
Kentucky 202
Kentucky Derby 202
Keyhole surgery 107
Kid Laroi 8
Kiely, Sophia 45
Killers of the Flower Moon 39
King penguin 138
King, Zach 94
Kitti's hog-nosed bat 117
Klum, Heidi 184
Koala 114
Komodo dragon 130
Komondor 150
Kramer vs. Kramer 35
Kukutali Preserve 185

L

La Voiture Noire 51
Labrador Retriever 151
Lady Gaga 24, 38
Lafleur, Guy 260
Lake 171, 229
Lake Huron 171
Lake Michigan 171
Lake Superior 171
Lake Victoria 171, 172
Las Vegas 13, 112
Latynina, Larisa 272
Laurence Olivier Awards 45
Leaf 163
Led Zeppelin 14
Ledecky, Katie 271
"Left and Right" 13
LEGO 82
Lemur 115
Leopard 121
Leroux, Gaston 42
Lesotho 243
"Level of Concern" 15
Lhotse 168
Lied Jungle 212
Lighthouse 207
Lightning 177
Lil Nas X 17
Liliuokalani, Queen 196
Lilly, Kristine 253
Lincoln, Abraham 206
Lincoln Park Zoo 198
Lion 120
Lion King, The 42, 43
The Little Mermaid 25
Living fossil 193
Lizard 130
Lloyd, Carli 253
Lloyd Webber, Andrew 42
Locust 143
London 44, 58
Long, Jessica 276
Los Angeles Hollywood Bowl 190
Los Angeles Lakers 244
Los Angeles Philharmonic 190
Los Angeles Rams 30
The Lost City 38
Louisiana 177, 203
Lover 9
Lover's Deep submarine hotel 68
Lunar module 58

M

"Ma City" 7
Macaroni penguin 138
McLaughlin, Sydney 274
Maezawa, Yusaku 89
Magic 94
Maglev train 55
MahaSamutr 73
Maine 204

Maine coon cat 154
Makalu 168
makeup 16, 31
Malaria 144
Maletsunyane Falls 243
Malone, Karl 247
Mandrill 119
Maple syrup 230
Mardi Gras 186
Mariana Trench 166
Mario franchise 103
Mario Kart 103
Marvel Cinematic Universe 32, 40
Maryland 205
Maryland State House 205
Massachusetts 205, 206
Matilda 45
Mawsynram 181
Mbappé, Kylian 257
"Me Porto Benito" 8
Mega-fire 175
Melting Face 92
Mesoamerican Barrier Reef 169
Messi, Lionel 88, 238, 256
Met Gala 24
Methuselah 160
Mexican free-tailed bat 228
Mexico 73, 128
Michigan 207
Michigan Stadium 67
Mickey Mouse 184
Microsoft 105
Midnights 9, 21
Migration 128, 145
Minecraft 104-105
Minefaire 2016 104-105
Minions: The Rise of Gru 29, 41
Minitrailer 53
Minnesota 208
Minnie Mouse 184
Miracle Milly 153
Miranda, Lin-Manuel 44
Mississippi 177, 200, 209
Mississippi-Missouri River 172
Missouri 210, 218
Mitchell, Ed, Sr. 227
Mixed martial arts 238
MLB 251
MLS 252
Mobility scooter 53
Monkey 119, 124
Monroe, Marilyn 24
Monster truck 52
Montana 167, 211
Montana, Joe 248
Montreal Canadiens 260, 262
Moon 58
MoonPie 227
Moose 113
Moreno, Jaime 252
Morocco 88

INDEX

Mosquito 144
Mosquito Fire 174
Moss, Randy 248
Moth 143
Motorcycle 192
Mount Everest 168
Mount Rushmore 226
Mount Shasta 179
Mountain 168, 226, 241
Mountain ash 161
Movie 25, 29, 31, 33, 34, 35, 38, 39, 40, 41, 43, 95, 208
MrBeast Burger 106
Mudbug 203
Muhammad, Dalilah 274
Museum 58, 211, 215
Museum of the Rockies 211
Music video 15, 21, 91
Musical 42–45
Musk, Elon 87
"My Money Don't Jiggle Jiggle" 25
Myanmar 117

N
Nadal, Rafael 259
Nala Cat 97
Nano-chameleon 133
Nansen Ski Club 214
Narendra Modi Stadium 67
Narwhal 126
NASA 49, 56, 57, 58, 77
NASCAR 227, 263
National Historic Landmark 196
National park 167, 194, 235
Native Americans 185, 187, 206, 226
Nazaré 173
NBA 244
NCAA 245
Nebraska 212
Nepal 168
Nest 136
Netflix 6, 24, 27
Netherlands 255
Nevada 213
New Caledonia Barrier Reef 169
New Century Global Center 72
New England Patriots 249
New Hampshire 205, 213
New Jersey 205, 215
New Mexico 216
New River Gorge Bridge 233
New species 112
New York 65, 217, 218
New York Yankees 251
New Zealand 167
NFL 248–249
NHL 260–262
Nickelodeon 91
Nike 87
Nile River 172
Ningaloo Reef 169

Nintendo DS 102
Nintendo Switch 100
Nishizawa, Ryue 64
No. 1 single 12, 17
Nobles, Brandon 112
Nock, Freddy 241
North Carolina 113, 218
North Dakota 159, 219
North Korea 67
Norway 75, 242, 255, 272, 277
Norway spruce 160

O
Oakland Athletics 251
Oheka Castle 218
Ohio 220
Ohio Stadium 67
Oil well 221
Oklahoma 221
Old Faithful 167
"Old Town Road" 17
Olympic Games 238, 245, 253, 264, 265–268, 271–275
One Direction 13
"One Sweet Day" 17
Oneida 217
Orakei Korako 167
Oregon 161, 174, 222
Ortega, Jenna 24
Oscars 33, 34, 35
Oseman, Alice 27
Oslo 75
Ostrava Poruba 73
Ostrich 120, 137
Ovechkin, Alex 261
Owens, Terrell 248

P
Paisajismo Urbano 76
Pajitnov, Alexey 100
Palacio de Sal 69
Pan-American Games 265
Papua New Guinea 125
Paralympians 276–277
Paralympic Hall of Fame 276
Parker Solar Probe 57
Pear Blossom Festival 222
Pearce, Christie 253
Pelé 239
Pelosi, Nancy 185
Penguin 138–139
Pennsylvania 67, 104, 105, 223
Pensmore 218
Pentagon 72
Pepper 225
Pepper X 225
Permafrost 176
Permission to Dance on Stage 13
Persian cat 154
Persson, Markus 105
Pet store 147

Petit, Philippe 241
Petition 93
Petty, Richard 263
PEZ candy 192
Phantom of the Opera, The 42
Phelps, Michael 272
Philadelphia Zoo 198
Phoenix Mercury 245
Pickleball 239
Pilgrims 206
Pilot 49
Pink Sauce 185
Pinkfong 91
Plane crash 147
"Plastic Off the Sofa" 19
PlayStation 2 102
Plymouth 206
Poarch, Bella 94
Poison dart frog 131
Pokémon 98–99, 103
Polar bear 198
Pole-vault 269
Pondexter, Cappie 245
Pons, Lili 190
Poodle 151
Portugal 88, 173
Prague Castle 80
Prairie 201
Presley, Elvis 14
Primate 118
Producers, The 44
Prometheus 160
Pronghorn 120
Pumpkin 162, 208
Puth, Charlie 13
Puzzle game 100
Pyongyang 67
Pyramid 83

Q
Qin Shi Huang 78–79
QTvan 53
Quadruple jumps 266
Queen 87

R
Rabbit 148
Ragdoll 154
Railroad 200
Rain forest 165, 212
Rainfall 181
Rapinoe, Megan 255
Red (Taylor's Version) 21
Redwood 161
Renaissance 19
Renewable energy 64
Rennert Mansion 218
Reptile 132, 133
Republican Party 185
Reputation 9
Retweeted tweet 89

282

Rhaetian Railway 48
Rhéaume, Manon 262
Rhode Island 224
Ribbon-tailed astrapia 135
Rice, Jerry 248
Richard, Maurice 260
Rift Valley 166
Rihanna 16
Rip Curl Pro 270
Ripley's Believe It or Not! 24
River 172, 188
Robbie, Margot 38
Robinson, Jackie 195
Roblox 90
Robot 107-109
Rock pool 125
Rocket booster 56
Rocky Mountain National Park 191
Roller coaster 60
Rolling Stones 11
Rolls-Royce Boat Tail 51
Rolls-Royce Sweptail 51
Ronaldo, Cristiano 88
Rose Bowl 250
Rottweiler 151
Rousey, Ronda 238
Royal palace 196
Rubin-Rosenbaum, Zipora 276
Rungrado 1st of May Stadium 67
"Running Up That Hill" 6
Russia 65, 113, 167, 171, 176, 209, 272
Ruth, Babe 251
Ryan's World 36

S

Sagarmatha 168
Sahara desert 170
St. Helena 152
St. Louis Blues 262
St. Louis Cardinals 251
St. Louis World's Fair 210
St. Lucia 68
St. Luke Penny Savings Bank 231
St. Vitus Cathedral 80
Salar de Uyuni 69
Salt 69
Saltwater crocodile 132
Saltwater lake 229
San Alfonso del Mar 73
San Antonio Spurs 244
San Francisco 75
San Francisco 49ers 248
San Francisco Giants 251
San Jose Earthquakes 252
Sandcastle 81
Santalaia Building 76
Savanna 122
Savi's Etruscan shrew 117
Schneider, Amy 128
School bus 50
Science Museum, London 58

Scorpion 112
Scottish fold 154
Scoville heat units 225
Sculpture 81, 83, 226
Seattle 75
Sejima, Kazuyo 64
Sgt. Pepper's Lonely Hearts Club Band 14
Shanghai 55
Shapiro-Barnum, Julian 6
Shark 125, 128-129
Sharm el-Sheikh 73
Sheeran, Ed 11, 26
Ship 82
SHoP Architects 65
Shopping mall 72
Shrek franchise 41
Shrew 117
Siberia 121, 174, 176
Siberian cat breed 154
Siberian tiger 121
Sikhote-Alin Mountains 121
Silver 213
Silver Lake 179
Simpsons, The 26
Sin City Hustler 52
Sinclair, Christine 253
Sink, Sadie 6
Sitka spruce 161
Siwa, Jojo 27
Skateboarding 240
Skating 265-266
Ski jump 214
Skiing 214, 234
Skowhegan State Fair 204
Skydive Dubai 49
Skyscraper 65, 66, 70-71
Slater, Kelly 270
Sleep 114
Smell 134
Smith, Emmitt 248
Smith, Will 39
Smorgasburg 6
Snake 131
Snoop Dogg 13
Snowboarding 264, 267
Snowfall 159, 179
Soccer 67, 88, 238, 239, 252-257
Solar power 48
Solar probe 57
South Carolina 225
South Dakota 180, 226
Soviet Union 100
Space telescope 77
Space tourism 49, 86
Spacecraft 49, 58-59
SpaceX Dragon 49
Speed of sound 56
Sphynx cat 154, 155
Spider 140
Spider-Man 32
Sports Hall of Fame 195

Sports stadium 67
Spotify 8, 20
Springbok 120
Sprinting 271
Squid 115
Squirrel 117
Stadium 7, 67, 197
Staircase 105
Stalagmite 164
Stanley Cup 260
Star Wars 32
State fair 204
"STAY" 8
Steamboat Willie 184
Steel arch bridge 233
Steinway Hall 65
Steinway Tower 65
Stijger, Wilfred 81
Stinkbird 134
Storm Elliott 159
Strait, George 18
Stranger Things 6, 25, 31
Streaming 8
Streep, Meryl 35
Street-legal car 51
Stumble Guys 90
Sturgeon 171
Styles, Harry 8
Subway Surfers 90
Sun 57
Super Bowl 30, 184, 249
Super Bowl LVI 30
Super Mario World 103
Surfing 173, 270
Surgical robot 107
Sustainable city 75
Sweden 160
Swift, Taylor 7, 9, 21
Swimming 271-272
Swimming pool 73
Swinomish community 185
Swiss Alps 241
Switzerland 48
Sydell Miller Mansion 218
Sydney 64
Sydney Modern 64
Sydney Opera House 65
Symphony of Lights 66
Syria 158
Syrian Desert 170

T

Tahoe National Forest 174
Tallgrass Prairie National Preserve 201
Tamarack 179
Tampa Bay Lightning 262
Tarantula 140
Tariq 6
Tasmania 161
Taurasi, Diana 245
Teapot Dome Service Station 232

283

INDEX

Telescope 77
Temperature extremes 158, 159, 178
Tennessee 18, 227
Tennis 258–259
Tenzing Norgay 168
Terra-cotta warriors 78–79
Tetris 100, 103
Tetris 99 100
Texas 177, 228
Thailand 73, 117
Thanksgiving celebration 206
Theme park 60
Theroux, Louis 25
Thompson, Tina 245
3D-printing 64
"Through the Decades" 202
"Thunder Over Louisville" 202
Tibet 168
Ticketmaster 7
Tiger 121
Tiger shark 129
Tightrope walk 241
TikTok 6, 17, 24, 25, 94–95, 113, 146, 185, 239
Titanosaur 127
"Tití Me Preguntó" 8
Toltec civilization 153
Tomb 78–79
Tomlin, Chris 190
Tomlinson, LaDainian 248
Tonga 159
Tongue 123, 133
Tony Awards 44, 45
Top Gun: Maverick 38, 39, 40, 208
Tops diner 215
Toronto Maple Leafs 260
Tortoise 152
Touchdowns 248
Tour, music 7, 11
Train 48, 55
Trebek, Alex 28
Tree 160–161, 165
Trimaran 48
Trinidad Moruga Scorpion 225
Tsunami 159
Tsunami Surge 61
Turkey 158
Turkmenistan 171
Tusk 126
TV show 25, 26, 27, 28, 30
Twenty One Pilots 15
Twitter 87, 89
Typhoon 178
Tyrannosaurus rex 211
Tyus, Wyomia 195

U

U2 11
Ukraine 65, 113, 174
Ultimate Fighting Championship (UFC) 238
Umbrella 181
Un Biodiversity Conference 159
UNICEF 31
Unicorn 147
Universal Studios 29, 41
University of Connecticut Huskies 245
Uruguay 254
US House of Representatives 185
US Open 258
USA 209, 245, 253, 255, 264, 267, 271, 272, 274, 275, 276, 277
see also individual states
USC Trojans 250
Utah 229

V

Vaccine 144
Valley of Geysers 167
Van Geest Design 48
Vanderbilt, George 218
Venom 130, 131, 140
Vermont 230
Viaduct 74
Video game 90, 100–105
Vietnam 164
Virginia 205, 231
Vivian 180
Volcano 159

W

Wade, Lestat 105
Walker, Maggie Lena 231
Wallis, Quvenzhané 34
Walter Family Arctic Tundra 198
Wampanoag people 206
Washington 75, 232
Washington, George 205
Washington Olympics 199
Water coaster 61
Water lily 163
Water vapor 159
Way, Danny 240
"We Don't Talk About Bruno" 7
Wednesday 24
West Nile virus 144
West Virginia 233
Whale 127
Whale shark 128
Wheel of Fortune 28
White, Shaun 267

White House 13
Whole Enchilada Fiesta 216
Wicked 42
Wight, Rev. Henry 224
Wildfire 174–175
Willamette National Forest 174
Willemijns, Mathias 162
Williams, Serena 258
Williams, Venus 258
Wimbledon 258
Wingspan 136
Winter Olympics 265, 266, 267
Winter X Games 240, 264
Wisconsin 234
WNBA 245
Wolferman's Bakery 222
Women's rights 220
Wondolowski, Chris 252
Working day 220
World Dream 82
World Health Organization (WHO) 144
World Series 251
World Trade Center 241
World Vert Championship 242
Worldloppet 234
Worm 184
Worthington-Cox, Eleanor 45
Wyoming 167, 235

X

X Games 240, 242, 267
X-43A plane 56
XPeng X2 Electric Flying Car 49

Y

Yacht 48
Yangtze River 172
Yellow fever 144
Yellow River 172
Yellowstone National Park 167, 235
Yeoh, Michelle 33
YHLQMDLG 20
YouTube 6, 7, 10, 36, 37, 86, 91, 94, 95, 106
Yup'ik 187

Z

Zambelli Fireworks 202
Zendaya 38
Zero carbon 48, 49, 75
Ziolkowski, Korczak 226
Zoo 113, 120, 198, 212
Zorn, Trischa 276

PHOTO CREDITS

Photos ©: cover top left: FlixPix/Alamy Stock Photo; cover top right: Album/Alamy Stock Photo; cover center left: PRESSINPHOTO SPORTS AGENCY/Alamy Stock Photo; cover bottom left: Robert Gauthier/Los Angeles Times via Getty Images; cover bottom center: Kevin Mazur/Getty Images for Nickelodeon; cover bottom right: Entertainment Pictures/Alamy Stock Photo; back cover top left: Sipa USA/Alamy Stock Photo; back cover top right: mlorenzphotography/Moment/Getty Images; back cover bottom left: NASA; back cover bottom right: WIN-Initiative/Stockbyte Unreleased/Getty Images; 4–5, 8: Joseph Okpako/WireImage/Getty Images; 6 top: Jason DeCrow/AP Images for Green Giant; 6 bottom: ZIK Images/United Archives via Getty Images; 7 top: YONHAP/EPA-EFE/Shutterstock; 7 center: PictureLux/The Hollywood Archive/Alamy Stock Photo; 7 bottom: Drew Angerer/Getty Images; 8 top left: calvindexter/DigitalVision Vectors/Getty Images; 9: Rolf Vennenbernd/picture-alliance/dpa/AP Images; 10 background: Petra Urbath/EyeEm/Getty Images; 10 center: GDA via AP Images; 11: RMV/Shutterstock; 12: Jonathan Short/Invision/AP Images; 13: Collection Christophel/Alamy Stock Photo; 14: AP Photo; 15: MARKA/Alamy Stock Photo; 16: Photographer Group/MEGA/GC Images/Getty Images; 17: John Shearer/Getty Images for The Recording Academy; 18: Rick Diamond/WireImage/Getty Images; 19: Kevin Mazur/WireImage/Getty Images; 20: Victor Chavez/Getty Images for Spotify; 21: Kevin Mazur/AMA2019/Getty Images for dcp; 22–23: Dom Slike/Alamy Stock Photo; 24 top: Album/Alamy Stock Photo; 24 bottom: Stephen Lovekin/BEI/Shutterstock; 25 top: FlixPix/Alamy Stock Photo; 25 center: David Fisher/Shutterstock; 25 bottom: Shutterstock; 26 top left: PeterPencil/DigitalVision Vectors/Getty Images; 26 background: zaricm/Getty Images; 26 center: PictureLux/The Hollywood Archive/Alamy Stock Photo; 27: Album/Alamy Stock Photo; 28: Tyler Golden/ABC via Getty Images; 29: Collection Christophel/Alamy Stock Photo; 30: Focus on Sport/Getty Images; 31: Kristin Callahan/Shutterstock; 32 background: Gaudilab/Dreamstime.com; 32 center: BFA/Alamy Stock Photo; 33: Anthony Harvey/Shutterstock; 34: Jim Smeal/BEI/Shutterstock; 35: AJ Pics/Alamy Stock Photo; 36: Ryan's World; 37: Panther Media GmbH/Alamy Stock Photo; 38: Album/Alamy Stock Photo; 39: Scott Garfitt/Shutterstock; 40: Entertainment Pictures/Alamy Stock Photo; 41: Photo 12/Alamy Stock Photo; 42 top: Jimmyi23/Dreamstime.com; 42 bottom: Simon Fergusson/Getty Images; 43: ROSLAN RAHMAN/AFP via Getty Images; 44: Bruce Glikas/FilmMagic/Getty Images; 45: Nick Harvey/WireImage/Getty Images; 46–47: Andrew Paterson/Alamy Stock Photo; 48 top: YANIK BUERKLI/EPA-EFE/Shutterstock; 48 bottom: Van Geest Design and Rob Doyle Design; 49 top: Andrey Pronin/iStock/Getty Images; 49 center left: NASA; 49 center right: mystockicons/DigitalVision Vectors/Getty Images; 49 bottom: AP Photo/Kamran Jebreili; 50 center: Jeffrey Greenberg/UIG via Getty Images; 51: Jeff Spicer/Getty Images for Rolls-Royce Motor Cars; 52: Brad and Jen Campbell/Barcroft/Barcroft Media via Getty Images; 53 bottom: Jonathan Hordle/REX/Shutterstock; 54: David Taylor/Allsport/Getty Images; 56: NASA; 57: NASA/Johns Hopkins APL; 58, 59: NASA; 60: Iain Masterton/www.agefotostock.com; 61: Hurricane Harbor Chicago; 62–63, 66: Kanok Sulaiman/Moment/Getty Images; 64 top: Xu Jianmei/Xinhua via Getty Images; 64 center: The Shore Club, Long Bay Beach, Turks & Caicos; 64 bottom: Iwan Baan, iwan@iwan.com, www.iwan.com/Avalon/Newscom; 65 top: Michael Ho Wai Lee/SOPA Images/Sipa USA via AP Images; 65 bottom: Patti McConville/Stockimo/Alamy Stock Photo; 66 top left: Ratsanai/DigitalVision Vectors/Getty Images; 67: Eric Lafforgue/Art In All Of Us/Corbis via Getty Images; 68: Oliver's Travels; 69: Palacio de Sal; 70, 71: WIN-Initiative/Stockbyte Unreleased/Getty Images; 72: Beercates/Dreamstime.com; 73: Crystal Lagoons/REX/Shutterstock; 74: Su Yang/Costfoto/Future Publishing via Getty Images; 75 top right: bubaone/Getty Images; 76: Paisajismo Urbano; 77: NASA/ESA/CSA/STScI; 78–79: Chederros/www.agefotostock.com; 81: Ritzau Scanpix/Sipa USA via AP Images; 82: Edward Wong/South China Morning Post via Getty Images; 83: domin_domin/E+/Getty Images; 84–85, 101: Activision

285

PHOTO CREDITS

Publishing; 86 top: Larry Marano/Shutterstock; 86 bottom: Kyodo via AP Images; 87 top: STR/NurPhoto via Getty Images; 87 center: Nike Japan; 87 bottom: STR/NurPhoto via AP Images; 88: Harry Langer/DeFodi Images via Getty Images; 89 top right: Aflo/Shutterstock; 89 main: Ejevica/Dreamstime.com; 90: Seemanta Dutta/Alamy Stock Photo; 91: Stephen Chung/Alamy Stock Photo; 93: Erik McGregor/LightRocket via Getty Images; 94: gotpap/Bauer-Griffin/GC Images/Getty Images; 95: Jay L Clendenin/Los Angeles Times/Shutterstock; 96: The Photo Access/Alamy Stock Photo; 97: Amanda Edwards/WireImage/Getty Images; 98–99: Hansons Auctioneers/MEGA/Newscom; 100: Normadesmond/Dreamstime.com; 102: Asiaselects/Alamy Stock Photo; 103: Stephen Lam/Getty Images; 104–105: theodore liasi/Alamy Stock Photo; 106: Kevin Mazur/Getty Images for Nickelodeon; 107: CMR Surgical; 108–109: Andreas Muehlbauer, Furth im Wald; 110–111, 121: Tom Brakefield/DigitalVision/Getty Images; 112 top: Prakrit Jain; 112 bottom: Brandon Nobles and Cody Clark of Jeffrys Farm (Follow us on IG @Jeffrys_farm); 113 top: Mustafa Ciftci/Anadolu Agency via Getty Images; 113 center: Alaska_icons/iStock/Getty Images; 113 bottom: DustinSafranek/iStock/Getty Images; 114 top left: Sudowoodo/iStock/Getty Images; 114 main: Martin Harvey/The Image Bank/Getty Images; 115: Nicholas Bergkessel, Jr./SCIENCE SOURCE; 116: Steve Bloom Images/SuperStock; 117: Steve Downeranth/Pantheon/SuperStock; 118: NHPA/SuperStock; 120 main: Gallo Images/The Image Bank/Getty Images; 120 icon: Krustovin/Dreamstime.com; 120 icon: filo/DigitalVision Vectors/Getty Images; 120 icon: Wectors/Dreamstime.com; 120 icon: D_A_S_H_U/iStock/Getty Images; 122–123: Art Wolfe/Stone/Getty Images; 125: Images & Stories/Alamy Stock Photo; 126: Bryan & Cherry Alexander/SCIENCE SOURCE; 127: Franco Banfi/WaterFrame/www.agefotostock.com; 129: Tobias Friedrich/WaterFrame/www.agefotostock.com; 130: Ksumano/Dreamstime.com; 132: William D. Bachman/SCIENCE SOURCE; 133: dpa picture alliance archive/Alamy Stock Photo; 134: nikpal/iStock/Getty Images; 135: Tim Laman/Minden Pictures; 136: Chris Knightstan/Pantheon/SuperStock; 137: Fabian Von Poser/imageBROKER/Shutterstock; 138–139: Raimund Linke/The Image Bank/Getty Images; 140: Karin Pezo/Alamy Stock Photo; 141: Satoshi Kuribayashi/Nature Production/Minden Pictures; 142: Piotr Naskrecki/Minden Pictures; 143: Stephen Dalton/Minden Pictures/SuperStock; 144: SURAPOL USANAKUL/Alamy Stock Photo; 145: Saurav Karki/iStock/Getty Images; 146 top: Homeward Bound Pet Adoption Center; 146 bottom: Courtesy of Taylor Blake/Knuckle Bump Farms; 147 top: Los Angeles County Animal Care and Control via AP Images; 147 center: HAWS Staff; 147 bottom: AP Photo/Diane Bondareff; 148: Kate Kunath/Photodisc/Getty Images; 149: Allan Hutchings/Shutterstock; 150: AP Photo/Mary Altaffer; 151: mlorenzphotography/Moment/Getty Images; 152: mark phillips/Alamy Stock Photo; 153 top: Hsc/Dreamstime.com; 156–157, 164–165: Geng Xu/iStock/Getty Images; 158 top: Kent Porter/The Press Democrat via AP Images; 158 bottom: AP Photo/Can Ozer; 159 top: EyePress News/Shutterstock; 159 center: JOED VIERA/AFP via Getty Images; 159 bottom: ANDREJ IVANOV/AFP via Getty Images; 160 top left: Ratsanai/DigitalVision Vectors/Getty Images; 160 main: p-orbital/iStock/Getty Images; 162: THOMAS KIENZLE/AFP via Getty Images; 163: SuperStock/www.agefotostock.com; 166: Operation IceBridge/NASA; 167: Idamini/Alamy Stock Photo; 169: Auscape/Universal Images Group via Getty Images; 170: Valentin Armianu/Dreamstime.com; 171: NASA image by Jeff Schmaltz, MODIS Rapid Response Team; 172: Ahmed El Araby/iStock/Getty Images; 173: AP Photo/Armando Franca; 174–175: THIBAUD MORITZ/AFP via Getty Images; 176: NASA Earth Observatory images by Jesse Allen; 178: Edu Botella/Europa Press via Getty Images; 179: CampPhoto/Getty Images; 180: Nadine Spires/Dreamstime.com; 181: Amos Chapple/Shutterstock; 182–183, 188: Anthony Grisham/EyeEm/Getty Images; 184 top: Stephen Lovekin/Shutterstock; 184 bottom: PictureLux/The Hollywood Archive/Alamy Stock Photo; 185 top: Ken Cedeno/UPI/Shutterstock; 185 center: CEO Photography; 185

bottom: capecodphoto/E+/ Getty Images; 186 top left: Anson_iStock/iStock/Getty Images; 186 main: Dan Anderson via ZUMA Wire/ Newscom; 187: Joe Raedle/ Getty Images; 190: EuroStyle Graphics/Alamy Stock Photo; 191: aznature/Getty Images; 192: Randy Duchaine/Alamy Stock Photo; 193: Newman Mark/www.agefotostock.com; 194: Michael S. Nolan/ BluePlanetArchive; 196: AP Photo/Lucy Pemoni; 197: Steve Conner/Icon SMI/Corbis via Getty Images; 199: Buyenlarge/ Getty Images; 200: Don Smetzer/Alamy Stock Photo; 201: Wolfgang Kaehler/ LightRocket via Getty Images; 202: Stephen J. Cohen/Getty Images; 203: John Cancalosi/ Pantheon/SuperStock; 204: Diane Labombarbe/ DigitalVision Vectors/Getty Images; 205 center: Djahan/ iStock/Getty Images; 208: AP Photo/Aaron Lavinsky/Star Tribune; 209: Richard Finkelstein for the USA IBC; 210: Historic Collection/Alamy Stock Photo; 211: Edgloris E. Marys/www.agefotostock.com; 212: Robert_Ford/iStock/Getty Images; 213: REUTERS/Alamy Stock Photo; 214: Nansen Ski Club; 215: Loop Images/UIG via Getty Images; 216 bottom: Visit Las Cruces; 217: Tina Pomposelli; 218 top: AP Photo/ Alan Marler; 218 bottom: siraanamwong/iStock/Getty Images; 220: Library of Congress; 221: joel zatz/Alamy Stock Photo; 222: Courtesy of Wolferman's Bakery™; 223: AP Photo/Matt Rourke; 224: Jerry Coli/Dreamstime.com; 225: Ed Currie/PuckerButt Pepper Company; 226: Sergio Pitamitz/ robertharding/Newscom; 228: Fritz Poelking/www.agefotostock.com; 229: Christian Heeb/www.agefotostock.com; 230: Raulersongirlstravel/iStock/ Getty Images; 231: Courtesy of National Park Service, Maggie L. Walker National Historic Site; 232: Kevin Schafer/ Photolibrary/Getty Images; 234: AP PHOTO/PAUL M. WALSH; 235: Richard Maschmeyer/www.agefotostock.com; 236–237, 271: Tom Pennington/Getty Images; 238 top: George Napolitano/MediaPunch/IPX/ AP Images; 238 bottom: Shaun Botterill/FIFA via Getty Images; 239 top: Rolls Press/Popperfoto via Getty Images; 239 center: Arden S. Barnes/For The Washington Post via Getty Images; 239 bottom: Jp Waldron/CSM/Shutterstock; 240 top left: pop_jop/ DigitalVision Vectors/Getty Images; 240 main: Streeter Lecka/Getty Images; 241: Gian Ehrenzeller/EPA/Shutterstock; 242: Tony Donaldson/Icon SMI/ Newscom; 243: How Ridiculous; 244: Ronald Martinez/Getty Images; 245: AP Photo/Elaine Thompson; 246–247: Harry How/Getty Images; 248: AP Photo/Greg Trott; 249: ERIK S LESSER/ EPA-EFE/Shutterstock; 250: Kevork Djansezian/Getty Images; 251: Jed Jacobsohn/ Getty Images; 252: Scott Winters/Icon Sportswire via AP Images; 253: Guang Niu/Getty Images; 254: AP Photo; 255: AP Photo/David Vincent; 256: FRANCK FIFE/AFP via Getty Images; 257: Sebastian Frej/MB Media/Getty Images; 258: Adam Pretty/Getty Images; 259: Jean Catuffe/Getty Images; 260: Bruce Bennett Studios/Getty Images; 261: Rocky Widner/Getty Images; 262: Bruce Bennett Studios/ Getty Images; 263: Jared C. Tilton/Getty Images; 264: Andrew Milligan/PA Images via Getty Images; 265: The World of Sports SC/Shutterstock; 266: MARCO BERTORELLO/AFP/ Getty Images; 267: The Yomiuri Shimbun via AP Images; 268: Aflo Co. Ltd./Alamy Stock Photo; 269: Oleksiewicz/ PressFocus/Shutterstock; 270: Koji Hirano/Getty Images; 272: Mitchell Gunn/Dreamstime.com; 273: Robert Gauthier/Los Angeles Times via Getty Images; 274: AP Photo/Morry Gash; 275: Stuart Robinson/ Express Newspapers via AP Images; 276: ARIS MESSINIS/ AFP/Getty Images; 277: Raphael Dias/Getty Images; 288: Courtesy of the Helbig family. All other photos © Shutterstock.com.

THE LAST WORD

DILLON HELBIG
BEST YOUNG NOVELIST

A second-grader in Boise, Idaho, went viral in 2022 after hiding a Christmas book he wrote at his local library. After eight-year-old Dillon Helbig snuck his story "The Adventures of Dillon Helbig's Crismis" onto a library shelf during the Christmas vacation, the librarians loved it so much that they put it on their system to allow people to borrow it. Dillon's festive book was written in a red notebook and accompanied by his own pencil-colored illustrations. It became a big hit, and by the end of January more than 50 people were on the library's waiting list to read it! His story has inspired other children in Boise to get writing, with the library getting many more requests from budding young authors wanting to share their work.